Professional Social Work in India

Revisiting the Past and Envisioning the Future

(From the archive of NJPSW - 1)

Editors

Kamlesh Kumar Sahu

Chittaranjan Subudhi

Indian Society of Professional Social Work
(ISPSW)

Professional Social Work in India: Revisiting the Past and Envisioning the Future

Editors: Kamlesh Kumar Sahu & Chittaranjan Subudhi

Publisher: Indian Society of Professional Social Work (ISPSW)
Registered office: Department of Psychiatric Social Work,
NIMHANS, Bangalore - 5600029
Secretariat: Mental Health Institute (MHI)
(Adjoining Punjab Police Institute)
Sector 32 C, Chandigarh – 160030
Email ID: contact.ispsw@gmail.com
Website: www.ispsw.net

Printer: Adroit Enterprises
SCO 41, Top Floor
Sector 30-C, Chandigarh – 160036

1st Edition 2021

ISBN: 978-81-952234-4-2

Dedicated to all the authors of this volume

Contents

Foreword

We started the National Journal of Professional Social Work as an official publication of The Indian Society of Professional Social Work (ISPSW) in 2000 with a lots of enthusiasm and hope that the journal will emerge as a platform for sharing research interests and findings and also helps us to seek a new directions in social work research.

It give us the immense pleasure to see the development in the journal particularly in terms of making it equipped with all current requirements of a scholarly journal.

Bringing this volume from the archive of the journal is a very cheering idea which will further strengthens the aim of the journal and it will be a new beginning for the ISPSW as a publisher of scholarly book.

Happy reading and learning with all the best wishes!

Date: March, 15 2021

-- Prof. T.B.B.S.V. Ramanaiah

Dr. V.N. Rao

Preface

The concept of 'Social Work' in India has been a long and ancient tradition. But as a profession it reached in 1936 from the west. In due course of times, several changes have been made in the course curriculum, syllabi and its practice. Eminent Indian academicians and practitioner have contributed a lot to the social work literature for its substantiate growth.

This edited volume is a collection of core social work articles that have been published in the National Journal of Professional Social Work, an official publication of The Indian Society of Professional Social Work (ISPSW). After taking the responsibility of editorship by the first editor the journal seek to become a truly online and open access and for the same it was required to upload all published volumes in the archive of the journal. That's why an extensive search was carried out to gather all previously published issues; while scanning and digitalizing the papers it was observed that some papers are on the common theme and it will give a in-depth insight on that particular topic if bring together; which was beyond the scope of a journal so, this book was conceptualized. The second editor took the pain of screening papers, OCR scanning, typesetting, and proofreading; due to the limited resource all these works had to do by himself.

The volume has five scholarly articles from those eminent professional social works who are no more with us (except the two authors of chapter two) but their wisdom is. It is humble effort to spread their knowledge and teachings which is a tribute to them.

Chapter one by Dr. M. Chandrasekhar Rao discusses about the principles of professional social work practice in India. In chapter two, the authors Dr. K Satyanarayana, Dr. Koteswar Raju, and Prof. B R K Raju have discussed about the revising social work practice in India. Chapter three by Prof. Rajeshwar Prasad discuss about the current situation of social work profession in India. Chapter four by Prof. Surendra Singh focuses on need and methodologies for development of knowledge for professional social work practice in India. Chapter five by Prof. Rajeshwar Prasad discuses about on different theories in social work vs. social work theory: predicament for profession and indigenization for possible curriculum change and practice reorientation.

All the chapters are critically evaluated the social work practicum in India and its growth and future perspective. The chapters will ignite the research and practice skills among young social workers' mind.

We would like to express our heartfelt gratitude to the founder editor in chief and editor, the president ISPSW and EC members for granting the permission to republish the papers and their voluble contribution in many ways to bring this volume.

Date: March 12, 2021

– *Kamlesh Kumar Sahu & Chittaranjan Subudhi*

1. PRINCIPLES OF PROFESSIONAL SOCIAL WORK PRACTICE IN INDIA

Dr. M. Chandrasekhar Rao[1]

Professionalism in Social Work has been an important issue ever since the inception of the field in the West. The Social Work educators and practitioners are concerned with the core elements of professionalism in Social Work. The "Six Criteria" of profession as proclaimed first by Abraham Flexner in 1915 has been subjected to differential interpretations (Austin, 1983) and re-interpretations even in the recent times (Morris, 2005). The seventy year old Social Work in India needs to ensure certain standards in professional training and practice of novice social workers.

Social Evolutionary Perspective

In this dynamic society, many young and unfamiliar professions are continuously moving their social positions by constantly updating their professional goals in response to changing needs of the society. Moreover, it is often evident that some major concerns of the field of Social Work are getting diluted due to the 'Social Side' of many other sectors such as health, education, industry and even

---

[1] *Late, Additional Professor, Department of Psychiatric Social Work, NIMHANS, Bangalore*

the business world. The Social Work practice is, thus, considered as complementary to many other practices, which affects its position in the hierarchy of professions. The field of Social Work has to consider if it is necessary to modify the traditional concerns and practice elements of Social Work in order to meet the demands of the society.

Theory-Practice Integration

Every profession revolves around a reciprocal exchange of knowledge from basic theories and realistic paradigms of practice. The theoretical knowledge base is continuously set and reset through the process of conceptualization, construction, formulation and empirical testing of theories. The practice wisdom rests completely upon the 1) Availability of practice settings and materials for practice and 2) Involvement of professionals with their armamentarium of methods, techniques, skills and values. A perfect match between the theoretical knowledge and practice wisdom make the professional practice a reality. The field of social work in India needs to formulate its theories of and theories for practice in order to make the field more indigenized. Further, it is import, that there is a link between those theories of social work educators and the practice knowledge (methods and techniques) of social work practitioners (Goldstein, 1990). This requires operationalization of the theories and conceptualization of practice. The resultant practice-theory integration is the reality of social work profession.

School-Agency Inseparability

There has been mushrooming of Schools of Social Work in India leading to debate among the Social Work educators over its pros and cons. Establishment of schools of social work may be essential for the evolution of social work profession. However, it is equally important to ensure the availability of social work practice settings in the society so that these can be utilized as field work agencies and as service delivery systems. The social work education in India needs to play an active role in the development, implementation and evaluation of various social welfare activities especially involving the trained social workers. The social work practitioners working in various settings must contribute their experiential knowledge to the field work supervision as well as to the theory development. Similarly, the social work educators need to examine the applicability of social Work theories in the practice settings. These schools can also conduct refresher courses for continuing professional development of the social work practitioners and educators. On the whole, the social work trainees must feel that they had professional training than teaching in social work and that both the classroom and field work agency are inseparable in nature.

Professional Conviction

The general premise of any profession is that its practice requires an intensive training. It insists that the practice done by the professional is distinct from that of the non-professional. The social work trainers and trainees need to have such a conviction that the course is different from other disciplines and the field work in social work education is an essential component of professional social work training. The social work practitioners and educators must develop and use professional language.

Professional Affiliation

It is equally important that the social workers in India need to realize the long term benefits of their affiliation to professional associations such as Indian Society of Professional Social Work. The professional bodies of social workers need to set code of conduct and ethical standards for social work practice, education and research in India as well as protect the needs and rights of professional social workers. Thus a mere degree of qualification does not guarantee the professionalism in social work practice. It has to be reflected in the nature of training, practice and research of social work in India. The novice social workers have to turn the current scenario of social work towards the new horizons of Professional Social Work.

References

Austin, D.M. (1983). The Flexner Myth and History of Social Work, *Social Science Review, 57* (3), 357-377.

Goldstein, H. (1990). The Knowledge Base of Social Work Practice. Theory, Wisdom Analogue or Art? *Families in Society, 71* (1), 32 - 43.

Morries, P. M. (2005). *A Gadamerian inquiry of Abraham Flexner's 1915 speech. Is Social Work a Profession?* (Doctoral dissertation), Virgina Common Wealth University, School of Social Work, Richmond.

2. RE-VISITING SOCIAL WORK

Dr. K Satyanarayana[1], *Dr. Koteswar Raju*[2], *Prof. B R K Raju*[3]

Social work seeks to enhance the social functioning of individuals singly and in groups, by activities focused on their social relationships which constitute the interaction between man and his environment. These activities can be grouped into three functions: restoration of impaired capacity, provision of individual and social resources, and prevention of social dysfunction (Warner, 1959, p.54).

As a service, social work is very old, but as a profession very new. Social work profession may be defined as the application of knowledge and techniques derived from many fields of art and science to the solution of the social problems besetting individuals, groups and communities. Social Work once thought of a basket-on-the-arm assistance to the poor is now a discipline, scientific in method and artful in manner that takes remedial action on problems in several area of society. It ministers to families in economic or emotional difficulty. Social work is a professional service

---

Principal, KGRL College, Bhumavaram, (A.P.)

[2] *Principal National Institute of Social Work and Social Sciences (NISWASS), Bhubaneswar, Odisha*

[3] *Late Prof. of Social Work, Andhra University, Visakhapatnam*

Which uses scientific techniques to alleviate economic, social and emotional distress, among individuals, groups and communities.

People in distress, destitution, and deprivation have been helped in the past by individuals motivated by religion which assured salvation as the reward for charity. Humanism, humanitarianism, philanthropy, democratic ideology, equality of all citizens, regard for human personality and respect for the rights of others including the indigent, the handicapped, the unemployed, the economically disturbed and those I need from the basis for charitable work. The charitable work taken up by individuals and voluntary organisations came to be termed as Social Work in due course of time.

Thus historically social work was associated with charities and volunteer assistance to the needy, and the charitable and philanthropic work had come to he generally known as social work and its personnel were identified and designated as social workers. Social work can therefore be visualized as helping the needy, suffering from material deficiencies, physical disability, mental disorder or emotional disturbance. Social work is intended to assist individuals, families and communities in understanding and solving their personal and social problems (Sachdeva, 1992-93, p.12).

Thus the service ideal or altruistic motivation is an important and prominent trait in this profession. The service ideal has been viewed as the 'pivot around which the moral claim to professional status revolves' (Wilensky & Lebeaux, 1958). The best interest of the clients is more important than self-interest. (Shetty, 1996, p. 261).

Social work, as a professional approach to the amelioration of social problems, originated in western industrial countries at the end of the nineteenth century. Since then social work has experienced considerable academic growth. It has evolved a way of meeting human needs which is quite different from the approach of a person whose credentials for social work are just good intentions (Shetty, 1996, p. 259).

The visionary personality and the founder of social work education in India, Manshardt (1985), enunciates for the first school that was founded by him, that professional training in social work stands for soundness of essential principles of education, for flexibility of method and for a working relationship with the whole professional field that will give both perspective and depth to its educational programme. While the school as a graduate institution seeks to maintain high academic standard, it also seeks to be eminently practical, applying the best of modern social thought to the solution of the present day social problems. It believes that scholarly activities are not incompatible with simplicity and common-sense, and that the test of professional social worker is his ability to give himself in intelligent, skilful and disintegrated service to others. To be eminently practical, Manshardt (1985) propounds that the activities of a high grade school of social work fall into three general fields: (a) the academic curriculum encompassing adequate knowledge of human nature, appreciation of environmental background, (b) an adequate philosophical consumption of normal human relations and knowledge of all other available sources of relief, (c) practical dealing with everyday problems of social life.

This founding father of social work visualises certain attributes(virtues) desired in the social worker by saying that social worker in order to be prepared to meet effectively the multiplicity of complex situations in which he will find himself must have a much wider background than a knowledge of a particular type of work. He must develop the habits of thinking which will stand in good stead when he is confronted by a situation that is out of ordinary. He must be prepared to face each new situation on his own merits and without prejudice. He should combine within himself both the critical attitude of students and the enthusiasm of the man of action. He should cultivate reading habits which will serve him in good stead throughout his career (Manshardt, 1985).

He goes on to add that 'We no longer regard poverty, unemployment and social inequalities as inherent in the divine order of things. Every social problems has its cause or causes. If the cause can be discovered, the problem in most cases can be solved. It is the functions of the Scho0l of social work to seek to explain the course of social problems and to suggest methods of approach of their solution. As social worker to do all in our power in alleviate human misery, but this is not all. Our larger problem is the problem of prevention. And if, as we have reason to believe, our current economic, system is the cause of much social maladjustment, if then becomes necessary for us to be realistic, and to face our problem (Manshardt, 1985, p. 154)

In his words, the profession of social work is pre-eminently a profession calling for rich qualities personality. The individual who is in trouble who needs food, clothing, shelter, medical attention, legal assistance or help personal, ethical or psychological problems comes to the social worker for the aid. The satisfactory adjustment of such a wide variety of problems is a severe tax upon the abilities of the social worker. He must not only know how to get things done, but mist also be able to hold the confidence of his client while the machineries is being put in motion. To help men to hope when they themselves feel there is no hope is no mean problem. "We in this situation cannot 'make' personality. Your biological inheritance has had much to say about that question. But we can, I believe, help you to develop intelligent sympathy, social imagination and some of the inner qualities which will give you confidence, poise and balance. As academic curriculum which neglects personal values is not much worth." (Manshardt, 1985, p.5).

Essentially the social worker helps others to help themselves and the satisfaction derived from assisting people is the greatest of this profession. A person who loves people, takes interest in them and enjoys working with them, may well be justified in considering a career in social work. A social worker should also possess the qualities of tolerance and flexibility and to get along with the people with different backgrounds and to work with them realistically without judging them (Sachdeva, 1992-93, p.13).

The basic idea underlying the establishment of the school is that social work in India now reached the point where it demands fully trained worker with an adequate philosophy of social work, and the technical equipment essential to avoid both human and financial wastage (Kumarappa, 1985, p. 10).

The major part of the curriculum of most schools of social work deals with Social Case Work and its allied subjects. Under this heading come the great number of problems connected with family welfare-such as broken homes, individuals in need of advice, medical treatment, employment and interpretation to other members of their group. In the study of Social Case Work, psychiatric social work, medical social work, child guidance, vocational guidance, juvenile delinquency, probation and parole are included. Social workers survey the various processes by which the individual who has not achieved a satisfactory adjustment to the demands of life, is consciously adjusted to his social environment. The field is so vast that some schools give their entire attention to Social Case Work alone.

Though much of the social work is conducted by private agencies, a great amount of work in every country is still carried on by the State. For this reason the general field of public welfare administration studying government efforts to deal with public health, maternity and child welfare, the care of the blind; deaf and mentally deficient, housing, city planning, industrial welfare and the administration of justice are considered. Although social work in most countries has begun under private auspices, the trend of the times is more and more towards the development of public agencies supported by the public funds. Such departments of governments need competent administrators as well as able men and women who can do the rank and file work, especially that of individualizing and humanizing social treatment (Manshardt, 1985-p.3).

In 1952, when the American Council in Social education was established, the social work educational institutions adopted a curriculum policy statement emphasizing a broad generic sequence of study in: 1. Social services policy and programmes, 2. Human growth and behaviour 3. Social work methods of social case work, social group work, community organisation, social work administration and social work research and 4. Social work practice or field work. Till the end of the fifties, social work education was primarily limited to the two year graduate programme. As a result of a comprehensive study of curriculum in 1959, a revised policy statement was accepted in 1962 which led to the devclopment of und.er graduate programmes in social work education, thc decreasing role of specializations by methods, an increasing emphasis upon the field of practice and incorporation of additional courses on socio-cultural elements, community organization, social administration, social policy, social planning and social research. In 1971, a new curriculum policy was adopted but current educational programmes continue to reflect the dominant influence of the frame work set in 1962. Essentially, the curriculum of American social work education is based upon the principles, concepts and theories derived from the fields of psychology, psychiatry, psychoanalysis, psychodrama, group dynamics and other related branches of psychology. At the same time, it continues to be encircled with the dominant social philosophies of American culture which give an overriding importance to the case work method of working with people in almost all settings of social work practice. Perhaps, in no society social work has attained as much professional status as in the United States (Nagpaul, 1996, p.135).

Khinduka (1987) noted that social work has a well-defined philosophy and is based on a foundation of knowledge, although theoretically derived and empirically validated knowledge is not the only basis for social work interventions.

Gore (1965) has described five approaches of social work in India in the order in which they made their appearance: the religious traditional approach, the liberal reformist approach, the secular missionary approach, the ethical revolutionary approach and the professional social work approach.

The First Indian Conference of Social Work was founded in 1947 which played an important role in the growth and development of social work in India, but the objectives of the Conference were very broad based and included any helping activity and any worker from the helping professions. During the years 1961-62 two important events took place in the history of Indian social work education.

These are:

- The formation of Association of Schools of Social Work in India in 1960 and
- Emergence of a national organization of professional social workers renamed as the Indian Association of Trained Social Workers.

These Associations have not been successful in influencing new schools of social work to follow certain basic minimum standards for developing a suitable curriculum. For the growth of social work, there is need for standardization of the curriculum at an all India basis (Shetty, 19945, p.271).

Remedial Versus Developmental Approach

Social work education in India began some forty nine years ago (so timed then) as an adaptation of the educational programme in the United States of America, where social welfare services were meant to 'assist people in their adjustment to an industrial, urban and metropolis dominated social milieu' (UGC, 1978, p.16). Social work in the USA was developed to help the deviants of the social system, where basic needs were made available to all by the society through its economic development, supplemented by measures of Social security offered by the government.

Social work in India acquired the nature of remedial and rehabilitative measures for those who became victims of exploitation in the social system or who were not able to cope with the changing demands of life. Although in the later years, some efforts were made in the country to indigenise social work education to meet the needs of people, it hardly acquired the developmental bias of changing the existing socio-economic system. Theoretically, although social work education emphasized that socially created diseases must be socially cured, it never came to grips with measures to prevent social disorganization through a change of the social system. On the contrary, it worked within the prevailing social, economic and political system and acted in support of its functioning (Nanavatm1985, p.316).

Ironically in 1966, a year after the publication of the report of the First Review Committee, the theme of a seminar organised by the association of Schools of Social Work in India was "The Role of the Social Work Profession in Social reconstruction". Most of the papers presented in the seminar severely criticized the traditional welfare approach and emphasized the need for a developmental perspective. The subsequent debates and seminars since then seem to have persisted with the theme which is amply reflected by the report of the Second Review Committee.

The Second Review Committee on Social Work Education (1978) in its report stated that "an inquiry into the causes of poverty and the evolution of measures for its elimination was the responsibility of social work. Unfortunately (both in India as well as elsewhere), this emphasis was lost sight of in the early stages of the growth of the profession. It took up the cause of assisting people in their adjustment to an industrial, urban, and metropolis dominated social milieu rather than identifying the causes of poverty and working for its removal. This happened because Indian social scientist (including sociologists and economists) were prone to accept the western model of development for the elimination of poverty. Our model of social work practice and education were consequently based on an industrial, urban and metropolis dominated society… Social work education was thus based on an individual urban based model… The late sixties have revealed that industrialisation can't eliminate poverty even from the affluent society… It has brought to the fore the globe need to emphasise the teaching of social action, social policy and the social administration, since it is the social milieu and not only the individual that is the major client of the profession" (Siddiqui, 1984, p.5).

Social work, as a profession, emerged in western societies increasingly as an organised response to the social dislocations and problems that were part of the process of industrialisation. However, the emergence of the industrial state in the west has been based largely on the principle of economic and not social development. Social concerns in development, and the profession's is own directions, have tended to he subservient to the overall objectives of the industrial state. We have glossed over concerns about the just allocation of resources and the impact industrial technology on people. As professional educators and practitioners, we have often been co-opted by the demands of "modern industrialism", and have not questioned always stone of the basic "contradictions between modern industrialism and the ideals of human growth and development" (Stinson, 1979, p. 11-13). This is not to deny the potential contribution than social work could make toward a more humane, "just and productive industrial society". But it is necessary to acknowledge the fact that, to a large extent, "modern industrialism" has glorified individualism and there has been tendency to manipulate people as objects, with the resultant dehumanizing of society. "The human service professions, including social work, at times haves raised critical questions regarding this situation but, by and large, we have, perhaps somewhat reluctantly, acquired in this state of affairs in the industrial society" (Sander, 1987, p. 380).

In other words, is the structure of social work as it has evolved in the developed world relevant to the developing world? The developed world today is characterized by the existence of an infrastructure of public financed services which protect the individual against destitution and hunger, guarantee income, maintenance, aid to dependent children, old age assistance and a host of other services. While these services cannot ensure happiness, they certainly ensure survival, relative physical comfort and health. In this context, the professional social worker focuses on problems of adjustment and human relationships through skilled counselling, referral and the utilization of available services and the mobilization of new ones. His tool kit consists of his own professional self and his ability to use case work, group work, community organisations and social action as ways in which to help client whether the client is an individual, a group or a community.

The professional function of social work services is at once specific and general. It is specific in that it focuses on the maximum possible fulfilment of the client's potential: it is general in the sense that the potential fulfilment is not sector bound: i.e. not limited to income sufficiency, education, health or achievement of maturity in individual social relationships. Is this, or similar conceptualisation of the structure and function of social work, meaningful and relevant in the context of a developing society? (Gore. 1983, p. 2).

The United Nations brought out five surveys which identified significant developments and trends in the training programmes in social work in different countries. The surveys, specifically the third and the fourth, highlighted the limited applicability of the American Model of Social Work education and pointed out the need for promoting indigenous methods, curricula and study materials. In subsequent years, the United Nations Commission in Bangkok took several initiators dating back to 1964 to promote the development of indigenous teaching materials by establishing a working group consisting of well-known social work educators from the south Asian region. Moreover, the Commission also sponsored a training centre in September 1966 which offered social work teachers an opportunity to work together jointly so as to identify the main principles of curriculum on an indigenous basis, to incorporate cultural factors in the practice in the practice of social work and to develop teaching material including case studies reflecting socio-economic conditions of the region.

In later years the United Nations Centre for Social Welfare and Development in Manila held many conferences and seminars, involving selected representatives of Schools of Social Work for mutual exchange of views on issues and problems and for the development of indigenous case records and other teaching materials. It is true that based upon the proceedings of the conferences and seminars, several surveys and reports became available stressing the importance of the development of indigenous approaches and study materials (Nagpaul,1946, p. 140).

Although several decades have passed since developing countries, including India. have adopted the western model of social work education, the discomfort felt by the countries at the existing method was highlighted only after the failure of the last U.N. Development Decades. As a result, number of countries, and national and international level organizations have tried to correct the existing models of social work education, as well as develop alternate ones, as reflected in some of the following efforts (Nanavatty, 1990, p.312).

Social work in India is based on the American model in its approach and curriculum contents (Midgley, 1981). Social work essentially emerged in the western countries from their culture, traditions and values. The approach was more individual oriented, ameliorative, and suited to an urban, metropolitan culture rather than a vast, rural and poor country like India. The model of the social welfare conceived by the Indian national leaders of that time like Gandhi and Nehru was developmental, with prevention as the essential characteristic feature. Gandhiji's goal of social development was Sarvodaya, the welfare of the entire population. Nehru envisaged a planned change in society through technology and science and the upliftment of the rural poor through land reforms and community development programmes (Shetty, 1996. p.269).

The need for indigenous elements of social work education in terms of its philosophy, approaches, principles, theories and study material cannot be over-looked because working with people, studying social problems and administering social welfare programmes call for indigenous orientation and skills. The foreignness of social work education is so much all-inclusive and pervasive as reflected in its basic organizations curricula and the teaching material that most social work graduates fail to pursue careers in professional social work. Moreover, existing training does not prepare them to assume roles of leadership in the planning, formulation and implementation of social welfare programmes at different levels of practice and administration. If social work has to move towards professionalism in any society and has to become effective, it must have indigenous foundations incorporating, dominant cultural philosophies on the one hand, and projected goals which are being promoted on other (Nagpaul, 1996, p.142).

This urge to indigenise professional education was not confined to the field of social work alone. Many social scientists to the third world were dissatisfied with the adoption of the same theories and practice of sociology, anthropology and other social sciences that were developed in the west. With the growing strength of the social scientists and their greater involvement in national development plans came the realization of the limitations in the application of the existing professional education to the requirements of the prevailing national and regional milieu. With this realization, the urge for change became very strong (Nanavatty, 1990, p.311).

Also, the question of the relevance of western models, theories and methods of social work practice for professional education in other nations has become a matter of increasing international interest. Concerns about this matter take many forms whether or not, for example, western perspectives on practice are really responsive to the personal and social needs of the populations of other regions; the implications of built-in cultural bias; and whether it is incumbent on particular nations to develop their own orientations to social work practice (Mathews, 1981; Midgley, 1981; Kakar, 1982; Vokel & Vogel, 1973; Goldstein, 1986, p.149).

Though narrow balkanisation in terms of methods of social work has been considerably reduced and there has been a marked shift towards common base of social work practice with an integrated approach, yet even now, there is more than required emphasis on social case work and social group work. In a country like India, where even basic survival needs of a quite a sizeable section of the population remain unmet, emphasis has to be shifted to the methods of social action to bring about desired changes in social policy, plans and programmes to promote social development, social welfare administration (which may be renamed as management of social services to add to the effectiveness of provision of social services through application of modern management techniques). In community organisation and social work research greater emphasis is required to be given on actual problem solving methods and techniques through action research. Greater emphasis should be given on counselling which is being taught at present as a very insignificant part of the paper on social case work (Sigh, 1995, p. 21).

Siddiqui envisions that in the third world context, where the welfare approach was a nonstarter from the beginning, the prevailing social realities demand a developmental perspective. Facilitating a better access by the maximum number of people to the essential social services needed for their development, for obvious reasons demands, not only adoption of social action as a primary method of social work. It also warrants much greater efforts to make it more effective by undertaking extensive research and sharing of experiences to obtain greater clarity concerning the various dimensions of this dynamic process. The use of the process requires far greater clarity on the part of the students of its goals and objectives, the value framework and the strategies, than is the case with any other method of social work. In fact, social action can be termed as the most 'controversial' yet the most challenging method of social work (Siddiqui, 1984, p.7).

He goes on to add that Social Work Education today is faced with the great challenge of responding to the need for bringing about desired changes in a social system which generates a plethora of problems and conditions which obstruct the normal social functioning of the majority of people. It must, therefore, rise up to the occasion and give a proper response by incorporating the required social action content in the curriculum. The new curriculum should train the social work students in the areas, methods and techniques of bringing about the desired changes in the social system. It should provide them with an opportunity to learn how to participate effectively in the formulation and implementation of social policies and plans as also in the organization of programmes that may be of real use in effecting the desired changes in the existing social set up. It should acquaint them with the various ways and means that can be helpful in bringing about desired progressive changes in the functioning of various social welfare organisations (Sigh, 1984, p. 154).

As remarked by George (1975) there is a new role for social worker in addition to the supporting and case work functions, in the tom of political mentor, aided and abettor. From the agency oriented remedial approach, social workers are now called upon to deal with the larger social issues that retard social progress, cause social problems and debilitate individual well-being. Also, there is a need for social workers who would bring about structural and institutional changes, and acceptance of social change, social action and social development as the prime focus of social work profession in the present context. The professional social worker has a special responsibility to promote civic awareness about social problems and to enlist cooperation from different sections of the population for solving them or for minimizing their incidence (Nagpau1, 1972, p.407).

An inevitable conclusion that may be drawn from a critical review of the SCENARIO is that focus of social work in the coming years will be on the liberation of the marginalized poor in tribal and rural areas and urban pockets of India. The methodology of social work will be a "people centered" approach involving their conscientisation and thereby ensuring their participation in the process of liberation (Ramachandran, 1986).

And therefore, social workers cannot evade the responsibility of helping the deprived members of the population to overcome all obstacles to the exercise of their basic legal rights.... They should make efforts to bring about a change in some of the values characteristic of a society, or a major segment of it (Gore, 1969, p.65-67).

Already in the comments made so far, reference has been made to the developmental perspective in social work, its emphasis, for example, on resource development, its potential for humanizing society and for optimal use of resources. However, it seems necessary to make a few specific comments regarding this perspective, especially in relation to effective utilization of resources.

The challenge, then, increasingly in the future to move more into the broader arena of policy development, institutional change and humanizing development. This is not to abandon the traditional roles of social work, but to increasingly face up to the newer demands on the profession in the effort to intervene more effectively along with and on behalf of the people. "It is within this frame work, that we have to explore further the developmental perspective in social work and the challenge and opportunity. It provides for the profession, in the context of scare resources".

"It has been suggested that the future is not so determined that we should not feel so inept about our ability to influence its direction" (Lipset, 1980, p. 35). Despite the complexity, the change and the competing forces at work, people still have to increasingly be associated with grassroots activities, consumer groups and social movements. Herein lies the potential for change and optimal use of human resources. "We need broad based advocacy on behalf of people to influence policy decisions in the political arena. This necessitates also a radical and critical stance. Difficult choices have to be made by social workers ahead. The challenge is to go beyond the current debate and our preoccupation with technology, to an appreciation of a philosophic stance in dealing with issues of development and scientifically in humanizing development".

There are new developments ahead in which the profession has a significant contribution to make. Not the least of these is the contribution to the quest for an "appropriate technology" from a humanistic perspective for future economic development. There is the search for a new relationship with nature and human values. There is renewed interest in the possibility of evolving a new life style with "people oriented" methods of production and new patterns of consumption. The quest, as far as possible, is for "non-violent forms of technology", to contribute to development and for the optimal use of human resources (Schumacher. 1975). The contribution that social work could make in this context, along with other professions, will be significant, if we accept the challenge of the developmental perspective (Sanders, 1987, p.386).

People who would pursue the path of human betterment would want to alleviate poverty and physical needs that represent barriers to individual and social development, would want to encourage and assist people to explore and develop their spiritual dimension, would want to breakdown the many barriers that divide the human family and bring disharmony and suffering, and would want to help people to recognize the importance of nature and teach respect for it. Are these the paths which social work is following? Are these major foci of our social curricula? Are they emphases in social work practice? (Cox, 1994, p.315).

Cox goes on to add "If we look at the way in which social work often describes itself I think that we might conclude that the above issues are central concerns of the profession. For example the international code of ethics which social work adopted at the Puerto Rico Conference in 1976 unequivocally points in this general direction (Alexander, 1982). Its basic principles include

- Every human being has a unique value,
- Every individual has a right of self-fulfilment, and
- Every society should function to provide maximum benefits to all its members.

The US National Association of Social Workers' code is even more explicit in jointing in the same direction. It includes:

- The social worker should act to ensure that all persons have access to resources and services they require.
- The social worker should act to expand choice (freedom to choose) and opportunity for all persons, and
- The social worker should promote conditions that encourage respect for human diversity.

As pertinently pointed out by Cox, "if social worker's code of ethics and basic principles reflect the four dimensions am of the human condition, it is not so clear that kind practice and education do. How much space in our curricula is devoted to poverty, the spiritual dimension, inter group relations, or ecological issues? I think usually little. How many of our graduates engage in front line poverty alleviation work? I think few. Why are there no schools of social work in the five poorest nations in our region: Afganisian, Bhutan, Nepal, Combodia and Laos? How can the UNDP (1993) report that our government departments and NGOs fail to touch even the poorest 5 to 10 percent of the population? How frequently does our practice focus on spiritual or ecological issues?" (Cox, 1994, p.316).

The sooner the social work profession finds answer to these questions the better will be its professional articulation, of course with a developmental perspective.

References

Alexander, C.A. (1982). The international code of ethics for the professional social worker. Sanders, D.S, Kuren, O. & Fischer, J (Eds.). *Fundamentals of Social Work Practice*. Belmont, Wadsworth.

Cox, D. A. V. I. D. (1994). The role of social work in bettering the human condition. *Indian Journal of Social Work*, *55*, 311-311.

George, K. N. (1975). Foreword. T.K Nair (Eds.) Social Work Education and Development of Weaker Sections, *Association of Schools of Social Work in India*.

Goldstein, H. (1986). Education for social work practice: A cognitive, cross-cultural approach. *International Social Work*, *29*(2), 149-164.

Gore, M. S. (1965). Social *work and social work education*. Bombay: Asia Publishing House.

Gore, M. S. (1969). *Social work and its human rights aspect*, in Proceedings of the XIV International Conference on Social Welfare, 1968, New York, Columbia University Press.

Gore, M. S. (1988). Levels of social work provisions in relation to needs in a developing society. *The Indian Journal of Social Work*, *49*(1), 1-9.

Kakar, S. (1982). *Shaman, mystics and doctors*, New York: Knopf Inc.

Khinduka, S.K. (1987). Social work and the human services (18th Edition). In the *Encyclopaedia of Social Work, Vol.2*, USA: National Association of Social Workers.

Kumarappa, J. M. (2016). Training for Social Work. *Indian Journal of Social Work*, 46(1), 7-14.

Shetty, L. (1996). Professionalisation of social work in the United States and India. *Indian Journal of Social Work*, 57, 259-276.

Lipset, S. M. (Ed.). (1979). *The third century: America as a post-industrial society* (Vol. 203). Hoover Institution Press, Stanford University.

Manshardt, C. (1985). Education for social work. *Indian Journal of Social Work,* 46(2), 149-155.

Mathew, G. (1981). The concept of self-determination in case work: From a less used perspective. *Indian Journal of Social Work,* 41(4), 369-79.

Midgley, J. (1981). Professional imperialism, social work in the third world. London: The Chaucer press Ltd.

Nagpaul, H. (1996). *Social work education: Need for Relevance: Social Work in Urban India*. Rawat Publications: Jaipur and New Delhi.

Nagpaul, H. (1972). Social work as a profession in India: A Sociological analysis. *Indian Journal of Social Work, 32*(4), 384-411.

Nanavatty, M. C. (1985). Social work education and professional development. *Indian Journal of Social Work,* 46(3), 315-325.

Nanavatty, M.C. (1990). Changing pattern of social work education in developing countries with special reference to India- need for alternate models. *Indian Journal of Social Work, 51*(2), 309-321.

Ramachandran, P. (1988). Perspective for social work training - 2000 A.D. *Indian Journal of Social Work,* 49(1), 11-20.

Sachdeva, D.R. (1992-93*). Social welfare administration in India.* Kitab Mahal, Allahabad.

Sanders, S.D. (1987). The development perspective in social work. *Indian Journal of Social Work, 47*(4), 379 - 387.

Schumacher, E. F. (1975). *Small is beautiful*. New York, Harper & Row, (p.28.)

Siddiqui, H. Y. (Ed.). (1984). *Social Work and Social Action: A Developmental Perspective*. Humanities Press.

Stinson, A. (1979). Community development in an era of perspective search. *Social Development Issues*, *3*(3), 6-21.

Surendra, S. (1984). Reorienting social work education for social action In Siddiqui, H. Y. (Ed.). (1984). *Social Work and Social Action: A Developmental Perspective*. Humanities Press.

Singh, S. (2003). Future challenges before social work profession in India and required responses. *Social Work Education in India: Challenges and Opportunities, New Royal Book Company, Lucknow*.

U. G. C. (1980).*Review of social work education in India: Retrospect and prospect*. University Grants Commission, New Delhi.

UNDP. (1993).*United Nations Development Programme; Human Development Report,* New York: Oxford University Press.

Vokel, L. & Vogel, B. (1973). Social work in Vietnam, *International Journal of Social Work, 16*(1), 13-19.

Warner, W. B. (1959). *Objectives of social work, Curriculum of the future, curriculum study (Vol.1).* Council on Social Work Education, New York.

Wilensky, H. & Lebeaux, C. (1958). *Industrial society and social welfare*. New York: Russell Sage Foundation.

3. SOCIAL WORK AS A PROFESSION

Prof. Rajeshwar Prasad[1]

For any discussion on social work as a profession it will be expedient to examine some of the definitions of profession. Carr-saunders and Wilson (1959) observed that "the possession of an intellectual technique acquired by special training, which can be applied to some sphere of everyday life, forms the distinguishing mark of a profession".

Professions are no longer viewed as mere vocations having professed knowledge or intellectual techniques. Talcott Parsons (1958) viewed a profession as 'a cluster of occupational roles' in which the incumbents perform certain functions valued in society in general, and by these activities typically earn a living as a full time job.

The profession is also conceived as a medium of delivering services. Hughes (1963) is of the opinion that a profession delivers services - advice or action or both -to individuals, organisations or governments, to whole classes or groups of people or to the public at large. Denzin (1968), however,

---

[1] *Late; Professor Emeritus and Farmer Director, Institute of Social Sciences, Agra & Ex. President of ISPSW and IATSW*

viewed professions as 'social movements' in the sense that they recruit only certain types of persons, develop high elaborate ideologies and supra-individual values, own mechanism of socialisation and often attempt at proselytization to bring new persons in the field.

Goldstein (1974) related the professions with the specific needs, requirements and sanctions of society. He asserted that the final measure of the profession's identity lies in the explicit character of what it does in the fulfilment of a societal need.

From the structural viewpoint and particularly from the angle of status and power, Crowin (1965) viewed the professions "in terms of the set of ideal structural characteristics which they are supposed to possess, or as vocations in the process of achieving these characteristics".

Goode (1957) highlighted the interest orientation of professions and characterised these as 'communities without physical locus': its members have an identity; share a value in common; role definitions vis-a-vis both members and non-members are not only agreed upon but are the same for all members; there is a common language within the areas of communal action; it has powers over its members and its limits are reasonably clef though these are not physical and geographical but social; it produces, new generation, though not biologically but socially, through its' over the selection of professional trainees and by means of its train-contra1 process it prepares its recruits through an adult socialisation process.

The 'professions' in Europe were under the control of the church in the medieval period. They are now free from the church control and divinity is not the reserve of professional activity. Again, the professions are no more viewed as 'vocations having professed knowledge on intellectual techniques'; as is evident from the above discussion, professions are now understood as 'cluster of occupational roles', 'a community without physical locus', 'social movement', 'a service delivery system', 'a set of ideal structural characteristics', 'a configuration of actions entailing execution of functions required, and sanctioned by society', 'a class, stall; and power oriented group of people having specialized skills'.

Characteristics of a profession

Most writers while attempting to define 'profession', have in fad identified a set of attributes or characteristics that make a profession Flexner (1915), Carr-saunders (1928), Barber (1963),Talcott Parson: (1958), Stone (1961), Goode (1960), Greenwood (1957), and many others have given a number of attributes, traits or characteristics of a profession These may be summarised as : (1) determination of own standards 01 education and training which is usually long, extended and formal; (if, systematic body of knowledge that may be imparted; (iii) set of technical skills which may be specially acquired; (iv) more rigorous adult socialisation experience provided to the student learner in professions than in other, occupations; (v) enforcement of minimum qualifications for entering an(thus achieving professional status; (vi) code of ethics; (vii) settling minimum fee for professional services; (viii) professional practice after being legally recognised and most legislation concerned with the profession being shaped by that profession; (ix) some form of licensure, and licensing and admission boards manned by the members of the profession; (x), freedom of practitioner from lay evaluation and control; (xi) norms practice enforced by the profession being more stringent than legal control (xii) existence of professional associations and the members more strongly identified and affiliated with the profession than the members of other occupations; (xiii) formal channel of communication between the professionals, e.g., a newsletter, journal, meetings, seminars and conferences; (xiv) primary orientation to community interests; (xv) fulfilment of a societal need; and (xvi) rewards which primarily symbolise work achievement.

Caplow (1954) and Wilensky (1964) do not consider 'knowledge' or 'skills' to be of any consequence in the emergence of any profession or in the making of a professional. Caplow identified sequential development of certain characteristics that marks the steps in the professionalization process as: (i) establishment of a professional association, (ii) assertion of a monopoly over some of the services; (iii) development of a code of ethics; (iv) political agitation for certification and licensing; (v) control of training facilities; and (vi) development of working relationship with other groups. Similarly, Wilensky asserted that occupations begin to professionalise as soon as they emerge: (a) as identifiable specialisations; (b) are sufficiently in demand to sustain the full time remunerative employment of some number of persons; (c) acquire a set of technical skills and encourage the development of general principles that can accumulate into a body of presumed fundamental knowledge; (d) generate around these livelihoods, skills and knowledge, and a sense of identity with others similarly engaged in the specialisation; and (e) share the conviction that a necessary social function can best be executed through; the occupational group. Wilensky thus considers the 'knowledge' accumulated by a profession as a kind of 'presumed fundamental allot knowledge', more important is the sense of identity of the group engaged in certain modes of livelihood and a conviction that some necessary social functions can be performed by them alone. Caplow too considered 'assertion of a monopoly over some of the services' by a group important for professionalization.

It was in this context that Stone (1961) had aptly remarked that professions have become distinctly closed systems to such an extent that professionals do not believe that outsiders can judge the quality of the work they perform.

Fine (1967) also opined that neither skill nor knowledge is the criterion of a profession; in fact, their acceptance by the public is the key1 to professionalization process.

In this light, Freidson (1972) in his study of profession of medicine observed that unlike occupations, professions are deliberately granted autonomy, including the exclusive right to determine who can legitimately) do its work and how the work should be done. No occupation can prevent employers, customers, clients and other workers from evaluating its work, whereas the profession can declare such 'outside' evaluation illegitimate and intolerable. So, the professions sometimes not only become closed but also autonomous to such an extent that they may even surpass the authority of the society to the detriment of wider societal interests.

Types of Professions

In sociological and social work literature the typology of profession has been variously attempted. Carr-saunders (1955), Reiss Jr. (1955), and many others have tried to evolve a typology of professions such as: (1) The old established professions that are founded upon the study of a theoretical structure of a department of learning which is used in the practice of the art founded on it, e.g., Religion (divinity), Law, Physic (medicine), Pedagogy (education, higher education) and Aesthetics. (2) The new professions that have emerged due to the advancement in science and technology. Engineering, natural and social sciences, chemistry area few examples of the new type of professions. (3) Semi or quasi professions are those in which the theoretical study of a field of learning is replaced by the acquisition of precise technical skill. The examples of the quasi or semi-professions are nursing, pharmacy, optometry, social work, etc. (4) Marginal profession is a category made up largely of those who perform technical assignments associated with professional activities, e.g. medical and laboratory technicians, testers, illustrators, draftsmen, interpreters, inspectors, etc. (5) Would-be-professions are those vocations and occupations whose members aspire to get professional status. Familiarity with modern practices in business, government, etc., generally distinguishes this group. Personnel directors, salesmen, business counsellors, institutional managers, etc., are some examples of vocation' whose members aspire to professional status.

This typological frame makes it difficult to distinguish between a 'profession' and a 'non-profession'. Almost all the vocations and occupations claim to have a set of accumulated knowledge, special technical skills and service that is rendered to the society, recognition by the society, control on the members following it, etc., and hence aspire for professionhood. Corwin (1965) commented that a vocation's activities are better explained by its aspirations than by its actual achievements, and professionalization represents the efforts of a vocation to enhance its social and economic position and a drive for status in society. It may be seen that 'professional roles' are cosmopolitan and ecumenical whereas the employee roles are local and parochial. However, today the professionals do perform employee roles and not only the professions but even some of the occupations have nation-wide organisations.

There is no denying the fact, however, that even the most established professions do not have all the attributes of a profession, and there is perhaps no occupation that may not exhibit some of these and claim professionhood. Also, an occupation that has become a profession in one society may not have begun aspiring for the status of profession in another society.

Social Work as a Profession

The very nomenclature, 'Social Work', creates some confusion in the minds of people about which Goldstein (1974) observed thus: "The disadvantage lies in the semantic confusion of its title... The term social work when compared with the more exact labels of other professions emerges as ambiguous and non-descriptive, revealing only that it has something to do with human relations". Flexner (1915) though, as far back as 1915, has asserted that social work could not qualify as a full-fledged profession because it was not founded on a body of scientific knowledge, yet the debate whether social work is a profession or not, is still continuing.

MacIver (1931), Witmer (1942), Brown (1942), Clarke (1947), Hollis and Taylor (1951), Pollak (1952), Greenwood (1953), Fink (1955), Eaton (1956), Bisno (1956), Cohen (1957), Wilensky and Lebeaux (1958), Stroup (1960), Friedlander (1964), Feldstein (1971), Goldstein (1974), and many others have extensively dwelt upon the nature of social work as a profession.

Those who advocate social work having attained a professional status contend that since the time when Flexner (1915) expressed doubts about the professional status of social work, it has traversed through a long way of professionalization. Brown argued that social work fulfils all the requirements given by Flexner for a complete profession. Greenwood (1953) also maintained that social work is already a profession in as much as it has too many points to congruence with the models to be classified as such. Clarke (1947) also remarked that social work is a form of professional service comprising a composite of knowledge and skills parts of which are and parts of which are not distinctive of social work, which attempts on the one hand to help the individual satisfy his needs in the social milieu i.e., the environment and, on the other, to remove as for as possible the barriers which obstruct people from achieving the best of which they are capable. The Sub-committee on the Working Definition of Social Work Practice for the Commission on Social Work Practice (1958), National Association of Social Workers (U.S.A.) asserted that social work practice, like the practice of all professions, is recognised by a constellation of value, purpose, sanction, knowledge and method.

From the discussion on professions, it is evidently clear that an already existing occupation or an occupation group tends to professionalise for achieving higher status in society. The tendency toward professionalization of occupations is considered inevitable in a growing industrial-urban society. Meyer (1959) observed that "With science-based technology becoming more and more visibly the basis for important functions-not only in production, communication and distribution but also in the provision of medical and other services - the prestige of the science based professions has increased more rapidly than that of the professions based on scholarship, such as law and the ministry. The new professions have clustered around the sciences, and all professions, including law and the ministry, make overtures to science. The hazy line between science and technology has encouraged many occupational groups to aspire to professional status. Almost every cluster of occupations in the economy of industrial society is capped by an occupational group expected to conserve, develop and apply the fund of basic knowledge required to perform the functions to which the occupations are directed. Such an occupational group is an existing, or an incipient, profession."

It would be relevant to explore whether there existed a distinct occupational group solely performing the welfare functions in society that has, in due course of time, laid claims to a professional status. Earlier, welfare functions were discharged by church functionaries and they still continue to perform these functions in the parishes. There is, however, no evidence to show that a separate occupational group of the type existed in society. The emergence of such a group, indeed, is the consequence of capitalism, decline in the church authority, necessity felt by other professions for such a group of workers and taking over of welfare functions by the voluntary organisations and the State. And, it is recently that social work has made overtures to science and also laid claims over a technology of rendering services to the individuals, groups and communities. It is argued that for serving the people efficiently and effectively it is necessary to professionalise. Applying the community and process models of social work to the problems of recruiting, training, allocation and organist ion of professionals. Meyer (1966) concluded that professionalization can increase the ability of social work to solve the pressing social problems confronting our society. No doubt, social work is striving hard to move up in the hierarchy of professions but the constraints of professionalism will drive social workers away from social action and social reform (Greenwood, 1957).

There are, thus. Differing views on not only the status of social work as a profession but also on the every issue as to whether it should or should not be a profession. Whereas it is claimed that social work has attained professionhood and there has emerged a relatively homogenous professional community, it is contested too on the ground that there are conflicts within social work over concepts, objectives and techniques (Tony Tripodv et al., 1976). There are many others who either doubt or oppose social work gaining a professional status. Cohen (1958), for example observed that "social work has made progress over the last several decades, but has not able fully to cons convince the community that those who possess the professional skill deliver a superior service than those who do not; and that the community stands to benefit from it and should prefer the superior performance. The difficulty which has plagued social work in its development as a profession is that the social worker's dedication is to a degree shared by all good men and women. Most human beings have a deep need to be their brothers' keepers. Hence we all resist and resent the nation that the task of the social workers requires a peculiar combination of temperament, intelligence, training and experience. The result is that social work has had to notion that any man with love in his heart can do the job."

Cohen's (1957) earlier remark that social workers having professional skills do not necessarily deliver a superior service is not only true for the American scene but aptly characterises the situation obtaining in other societies also. In the Third World context social work has emerged as a stronger ally of the capitalists and other exploitative organs of society and has failed to face the real problems of poverty and exploitation of the masses. The Indian scene bears this testimony, and doubts as to the efficacy of social work in the solution of the problem of poverty have been widely expressed (Rageshwar Prasad, 1977).

Feldstein (1971) was critical about the process by which social work and other similar occupational groups have achieved greater professionalism. He gave four major arguments: (i) exclusion of many from entry; (ii) professional expertise is anti-democratic: (iii) professions attempt to influence public policy at the expense of 'people' and (iv) the professions have not provided effective services. His contention is that there is basic conflict between professionalization and consumerism.

Newman and Jerry Turem (1974) while lamenting about the course of professionalization of social work remarked that "it is a cause of despair however, that social workers, while indulging in rhetoric about their social responsibilities, often do not have even the most elementary regard for the mechanics of social accountability." And Scott Briar (1973) observed that social work as a profession is too ineffective as it is sliding from theory to theory, from technique to technique, but seldom grappling with the question of whether what was accomplished did the clients any good.

The Nature of Social Work Profession

There is evidently no unanimity in respect of social work profession and there are controversies in regard to its acceptance as a profession. As has already been stated social work is not an old established profession: it is rather a new and emerging profession with enormous contradictions. The pre-requisite of social work profession to operate in an agency setting limits its scope, scuttles its autonomy and snatches the opportunities of dissent and innovation. Federico Souflee Jr. (1977), labelled social work as an acquiescing profession.

Etzioni (1969) and Toren (1972) have classified social work as a semi-profession. Toren argues that social work practice as compared to that of full-fledged professions has under-developed theoretical knowledge; relatively low professional autonomy and authority of social work practitioners within the organisations in which social work is carried out; and a dyadic structure of the practitioner-client relationship and its insulation from the client's social milieu. "The first two factors are the main elements of semi-professionalism; the third is a structural property of the professional client relationship which, in conjunction with the two ormer variables, enhance the impact of semi-professionalism on social work performance and achievements (Nina Toren, 1972)."

Social Work as Profession in India

Social Work emerged as an occupation only recently in India and it is still struggling to achieve a professional status. The arguments of Indian social workers tread on the same path as those of the Americans to justify the professional status of social work. However, there are controversies in regard to the nature of social work in India. Sushil Chandra (1954), for example, avoided labelling social work as an occupation or profession and, instead, described it as a "dynamic activity undertaken by public or private effort in the implementation of social policy, with a view to raise the standard of living and to bring about social, economic, political and cultural well-being of the individual, family and the group within a society irrespective of its stage of social development". Gore (1965), on the other hand, characterised social work in India as a new profession, hesitatingly accepted as such by the Indian society, borrowed from the West (USA), and having concomitant consequences due to the borrowing on its own development. One of the consequences of this borrowing perhaps is that social work knowledge - theoretical frame, practice, methodology and social issues - are not drawn from the Indian context.

Social work profession is stigmatised for its identification with the backward section of the community. Quite a large number of social workers the past have, therefore, contended that since social work is not a profession of 'high status' in India, in order to raise its image and status ere is a need to discard the notion of professional social work being identified with the low income groups. For, it is commonly understood at the social worker's focus of attention is the backward and disadvantaged sections of the population. But such notions about social workers need to be discarded - the earlier the better - as modern social work has already lost its class character' .On the other side Rajeshwar Prasad (1976) asserted that "Social work profession cannot now afford to be an elitist profession; it has to relate itself with the real problems of the masses."

Hans and Kamla Nagpaul (1962) argued that on basis of application of most essential elements which form the bases of a profession, social work in India qualifies for the status of a profession and need to be recognised as such. Nagpauls, however, in their arguments could not establish the claim of social work for a professional recognition in the country on any empirical evidence. Wadia (1961) had aptly remarked that "Social work may claim to be a new profession with its emphasis in organised attempts to ameliorating human sufferings, but it cannot get away from its original moorings in the human heart..... Those who take up this work cannot make it a source of income and so any assistance that can be given by them can only be a matter of love and honorary service. This was social work par excellence".

Progress of Social Work in India

Thus, it may be seen that there is no consensus as to the exact nature of social work in India. This, no doubt, is a universal picture but the controversy is sharper in India due to historical and ideological reasons. In this frame of reference it would be apt to review briefly the progress of 'social work-profession' in India since Nanavatty (1968) attempted such a review in 1968, in the Encyclopaedia of Social Work in India.

Some points may be noted about the nature, extent and growth c social work in India. These are:

(1) Since the establishment of the Tata Institute of Social Science (founded as Sir Dorabji Tata Graduate School of Social Work) in 1936 there has been proliferation of institutions imparting education and training in social work in the country. In 1978, there were thirty-five School: Institutes/Faculties of Social Work (UGC, 1978). The distribution of the institutions is uneven in the country, e.g. there are eight such institution in Maharashtra alone and six in Tamil Nadu, while there is none in Jammu and Kashmir, Himachal, Haryana, Assam, Manipur, Bihar, Orissa, Arunachal, Goa, Pondicherry, Nagaland, Sikkim and Andaman and Nicobar. The economically backward areas and States with predominance of tribal population and agricultural labour do not have

any training institution. This reflects the trend of development of the profession which has not changed substantially in the last decade.

(2) Training institutions still continue to cater to the requirements of middle and big industries and personnel departments. The statutory provision in Factories Act, 1948, and the Rules made under it for employing welfare functionaries in factories have not only lent support to continued training in labour welfare' in schools of social work but it has also eased out other fields of training and specialisation of social work. The contradiction, however, continues that the industrial setting does not offer opportunities for the use of social work methods, and 'welfare functions' are hardly performed by this type of personnel. However, in the areas of personnel and industrial relations, a major challenge to schools of social work in respect of preparing suitable personnel for the industry has been posed today by State Labour Institutes and Schools of Business Management. Social work continues to have a monopoly over the supply of 'welfare personnel' to industrial establishments.

(3) The existing education and training of social work are not geared toward actual social work practice by social work professionals in their work milieu. The question whether we have a training programme chiefly in 'administration' or in 'social work' in our schools is still relevant. For example, one of the main objectives of the Tata Institute was to train "efficient administrators of social work enterprise" (Nanavatty, 1968). Most of the schools

prepare graduates for administrative jobs rather than the classical social work roles.

(4) There is a problem of sub-standard training facilities which has been further accentuated due to unplanned growth of training institutions, the lack of agencies suitable for field work, paucity of indigenous literature and dearth of suitable educators. These, with the weak infrastructure supportive of training and education in social work, have further eroded the credibility of social work education suitable for societal demands.

(5) The problems of lack of clarification of the role of social workers in various settings and uneven conditions of work still persist. For example, the roles of labour welfare officers; medical, rehabilitation and psychiatric social workers; probation workers; welfare administrators; and social workers in the field of population management are still confused and there are uneven conditions of work that exist in the private and public sectors.

(6) Doubts are widely expressed about the nature of social work knowledge as such; and the knowledge base of social work in India is subject of greater scrutiny and critical evaluation from the viewpoint sustaining the claims of social work as a profession. It must be accepted that a differential knowledge base of social work derived from India experience and material has yet to be developed. The main reasons are the lack of research activity in professional schools, absence of involvement of the teaching faculty in social work practice, irrelevant

role situations of the 'practitioners' in the field, etc. Field work supervision of the student - learner is done in the agency - setting whereas the agencies themselves are not well equipped for such a function. Although the type of problems that need to be faced by professional social workers in the country do not require an agency setting, yet the schools still feel shy it adopting other avenues or modes of field work.

(7) There are quite a number of organisations concerned with professional social works, such as the Indian Council of Social Welfare (formerly, Indian Conference of Social Work), a forum established by trained social workers for an interaction between 'professional' and 'nonprofessional' social workers in the country; Indian Association of Trained Social Workers (IATSW), formerly Association of Alumni of Schools of Social Work in India; Association of Schools of Social Work in India; Indian Society of Psychiatric Social Work; Labour Welfare Officers' Association; Probation Officers' Association, etc. However, the elements of organisation, solidification and control over the 'profession' and 'professionals' are yet lacking. There is neither visible control on the professionals nor on the schools, whereas these are distinctly evident in the cases of medicine and law in the country.

There are no doubt two journals, Social Work Forum of the IATSW and the Indian Journal of Social Work (Tata Institute of Social Sciences, Bombay), but a review of the material published in these journals does not really make these as representative professional journals. The 'professional communication' through these journals is too inadequate; Social Work Forum has not appeared for the last several years and the IJSW is not restricted to social work only. There appear stray magazines published by some schools whose publication is most irregular and of local interest. The Indian Society of Psychiatric Social Work and the Association of Schools of Social Work in India bring out bulletins, meant for the members. These serve a limited purpose of disseminating information and other relevant news to members.

Other Issues

It must be recognised that "social welfare as a profession grew in the capitalist societies at the point of time when the human miseries started multiplying as a consequence of capitalist exploitation. There was a felt need of 'professionals' to manage the spill-over of services dished out for the 'vulnerable' groups by the 'Humane', 'Welfare' capitalism" (Rajeshwar Prasad, 1979). India is no exception except for the fact that the beginnings of 'professional social work' were made in the colonial period itself. In many countries of the Third World the role social work has played in supporting the capitalist welfare state is being decried. In India social work has to discard this image to get people's recognition.

Other issues related with the 'profession' are: the development of a code of ethics, and public recognition. The code of ethics of any profession, more so the profession of social work, cannot be borrowed lock, stock and barrel; it has to be drawn largely from the traditions, philosophy and ethos of the country where it is practised. Public recognition will depend on whether the activity is in conformity with the local genius and milieu. Social work in India is a borrowed undertaking and thus it faces either opposition or neglect. Radhakamal Mukerjee (1965) had aptly remarked that "Social work is the youngest yet unhonoured and unacknowledged profession in India. It has no doubt grounded itself at different universities and research institutes in the country in the acquisition of professional skills and techniques in the various specialised fields of social work. But it has obtained neither social recognition nor developed a code of ethics grounded in a philosophy of social work and welfare".

Some other issues that need to be highlighted are social obligation of the profession to the legislature and society; communicability; development of 'professional self' without shedding the ancient Indian Concept of 'being and becoming'; development of indigenous social work values consistent with the aspirations of the toiling masses, and in conformity with the economic and political ideology enshrined in the Constitution of India; licensing, certification, registration and adequate regulation of professional practice in the areas where necessary; creation of an atmosphere where social work practice may not only he acceptable but actually established in the domain of private agencies in the country'. These issues, though very real, for the existence of the profession, have not been adequately debated.

The Future

There are very few studies in the sociology of professions in India and there is hardly any study of consequence on the profession of social work, hence it will be difficult to project the future of the profession of social work in the country.

However, it is evident that due to the strong social welfare traditions in India social work will not be able to assert its monopoly in welfare services. No doubt professional associations have been formed, but the identity of the professionals with the profession is so weak that for a long time to come these associations will not be able to exert any influence on society, and professionals will not be controlled through them. Due to diversity in the educational pattern, the profession may not be able to control the training institutions. Certification, registration, licencing and regulation of the profession will be non-issues for quite some time to come.

Since the profession under varied influences will not be able to shed away the Western model of education, training and practices, it will thus be difficult to evolve an indigenous code of ethics for 'Indian social work'.

Social workers have now increasingly started working in different settings: medical, psychiatric, industrial, rural, and correctional; however, a stable working relationship with related groups like psychiatrists, medical practitioners, industrial managers, etc. has not developed. Such a relationship is not likely to develop due to unclear roles social workers have to play in these fields. Undoubtedly, a sufficiently large number of persons will continue to be employed full time, but work situations are likely to be uneven and largely unrelated to social work education and techniques.

Although increasing concern was lately being shown for poverty and other mass problems, the profession will in all probability continue to maintain its elitist character, drawing its trainees from the urban middle class. Consequently, the rural and tribal sectors will not be served effectively by social work professionals in fields where they would be needed most.

Instead of professionalization of social work there is likely to be increasing bureaucratisation. So it will be hard to get public recognition or mass support for the profession for these and many other reasons.

(This paper has been recasted from his paper on Social Work as Profession in Encyclopaedia of Social Work in India, Vol. Three).

Note:

1. Unfortunately there is no verbatum record of the transactions of many a conferences and seminars of social workers in the country where such like views have been expressed freely. The author had an opportunity of attending quite a

number of such meetings and has used his personal notes on the subject.

2. For a detailed discussion about these issues see. S..V Ranade Administration through Private Agencies", Indian Journal of Social Work. XXVI (2). 1965; M.C. Nanavatty "Growth and the Problems of Social Work Profession in India", Indian Journal of Social Work, XXVIII. 1967; PT Thomas "Problems of Social Work Education In India", Ibid., XXVIII (1), 1967; G.R. Banerjee, "Social Welfare in Ancient-India", Ibdi.. XXVIII (2), July 1967; Hans Nagpaul: -Dilemmas of Social Work Education In India". Ibid; Chandi Prasad, "Nature of Social Work Knowledge And Teaching of Social Work in India", Journal of Social Sciences. Institute of Social Sciences. Agra University. Agra. Vo. 1, No. 2, July 1958, pp. 65-74.

References

Barber, B. (1963). Some problems in the sociology of the professions. *Daedalus*, 669-688.

Bisno, H. (1956). How social will social work be? *Social Work, 1*(2), pp. 12-18.

Brown, E. (1942). *Social work as a profession.* Russell Sage Foundation: New York.

Caplow, T. (1954). *The sociology of work*, University of Minnesota Press: Minneapolis.

Carr-Saunders, A.M. (1928). *Professions: Their organisation and place in society.* Clarendon Press. Oxford: England.

Carr-Saunders, A. M. (1955). Metropolitan conditions and traditional professional relationships. In Robert M. Fisher (ed.).*The Metropolis in Modern Life*, Doubleday and Co.: New York.

Carr-Saunders, A.M. & Wilson, R. A. (1959). Professions. In Edwin R. A. Selig and Elvin Johnson (eds.). *Encyclopaedia of social sciences*. Macmillan Co.: New York

Clarke, H. I. (1947).*Principles and practice of social for Appleton-century Crof*, Inc.: New York.

Cohen, N. E. (1958). Social work as a profession. In *Social Work Ye Book 1957*, National Association of Social Workers, New York, 1957. Also see his Social Work in the American Tradition, Dryden Press, New York.

Crowin, R. G. (1956). *A sociology of education: Emerging patterns of class, status and power in the public schools* (p. 221-222), Appleton-Century-Crofts Educational Division, Meredith Corporation: New York.

Denzin N. K. (1968). Pharmacy: Incomplete professionalization. *Social Forces, 46* (3), p. 376

Eaton, J. W. (1956). Whence and whither social work? *Social Work 1* (1), p. 11-26.

Etzioni A. (ed.) (1969). *Preface*. In the semi-professions and their organizations: teachers, nurses, social workers, Free Press: Glencoe.

Federico S. Jr. (1977). Social work: The acquiescing profession. *JNASW, 12*(5), 419-421.

Feldstein, D. (1971). Do we need professionals in our society? professionalization vs. consumerism, *Social Work, 16*(4), 5-11.

Fine, S. (1967). *Guidelines to the design of new careers.* W.E. Upjohn Institute, Kalamazoo, Mich.

Fink, A.E. (1955). The fields of social work. Henry Holt and Col, New York.

Flexner, A. (1915). *Is social work a profession*? Proceedings of the National Conference of Charities and Corrections, Chicago, pp. 576-90.

Friedlander, W.A. (1964). *Concepts and methods of social work (ed.)* Prentice Hall of India Pvt. Ltd: New Delhi.

Friedson, E. (1972). *Profession of medicine: A study of the sociology of Applied Knowledge.* Dodd, Mead & Co.: New York.

Goldstein, H. (1973). *Social work practice: A unitary approach.* University of South Carolina Press.

Gore, M.S. (1965). *Social work and social work education in India.* Asia Publishing House: Bombay.

Gode, W. (1987). Thin a community. *American Sociological Review, 22,* 194-200.

Goode, W. (1960). Encroachment, charlatanism, and the emerging profession: psychology, sociology and medicine. *American Sociological Review*, *25*, 902-914.

Greenwood, E. (1953). *Toward a sociology of social work, research department*, (Special Report No. 37). Regional Welfare Planning Council of Metropolitan Los Angeles.

Greenwood, E. (1957). Attributes of a profession. *Social Work, 11*(3), 45-55.

Hughes, E. C. (1963). Professions. *Daedaulus, 19* (4), 655-68.

Hollis, E. & Alice, L. (1951). *Social work education in the United States*. Columbia University Press: New York.

Hans, N. & Kamla, N. (1962). Social work education in India. In S. K. Khenduka (Eds.) Social Work in India (p. 164-80), Sarvodaya Sahitay Samaj, Jaipur:

Mans Nagpaul. The Study of Indian Society (A Sociological Analysis of Social Welfare and Social Work Education) A doctoral thesis of Institute of Social Sciences, Agra, S. Chand & Co., New Delhi.

Hughes, E. C. (1963). Professions. *Daedaulus*, *19* (4), 655-68.

Maclver, R.M. (1963). *The contributions of sociology to social work*. Columbia University Press: New York.

Myer, H. J. (1959). Professionalization and social work. In Alfred J. Kohn (Eds.). *Issues in American social work* (p. 321-22). Columbia University Press: New York.

Meyer, H. J. (1966). Social work profession as a community or social movement. In Edward E. Sehwartze (Eds.) *Manpower in social welfare: Research perspectives* (p. 66-80). New York.

Nanavatty, M.C. (1968). The social work profession. In: *Encyclopaedia of social work in India* (Vol. two), (The Planning Commission), Publication Division, Government of India. New Delhi.

National Association of Social Workers, U.S.A., (NASW) (1958). *Sub-Committee on the working definition of social work practice for the commission on social work practice*, quoted in Toward Classification and Improvement of Social Work Practice, by Harriet M. Bartlett, Social Work, III. April.

Newman, E., & Jerry, T. (1974). Crises of accountability. *Social Work*, 19(1), 5-16.

Pollak, O. (1952). The Culture of Psychiatric Social Work. *Journal of Psychiatric Social Work*, *21*(4), 160-165.

Radhakamal, M. (1965). Social Welfare Administration, *Indian Journal Social Work, 26(2)*, 173-181.

Rajeshwar, P. (1976). Public Social Welfare Set-up In Uttar Pradesh; Analysis. In Rajeshwar Prasad (ed.), Social Administration in Uttar Pradesh in the Context of National Development, Institute of Social Sciences, Agra, p. 65.

Prasad, R. (1977). Challenges of Poverty and the Social Work Curriculum. Journal of Social Research, Ranchi, 20(1), 79-89.

Prasad, R. (1979). Social Policy: An analysis of Social Policy Courses Social Work and other Social Sciences, National Seminar on Social Polk Association of Schools of Social Work in India, Hyderabad, June 16-1, 1979.

Reiss Jr., Albert J. "Occupational Mobility or Professional Workers' American Sociological Review, XXI, Dec. 1955, pp. 693-94.

Scott Briar, "Effective Social Work Intervention in Direct Practice Implications for Education", paper presented at the annual meeting of the Council on Social Work Education, San Fransisco, California, U.S.A., Fel 1973.

Stone, Robert C., in Readings in Contemporary American Sociology, Josepl S. Rouchek (ed.), Little Field, Adams & Co., Paterson, New Jersey, p. 494 1961.

Stroup, H.H., Social Work - An Introduction to the Field, American Bool Co., New York, 1960.

Sushil Chandra, Social Work in Uttar Pradesh, a brochure published at the time of the Conference of the Indian Conference of Social Work, J.K. Institute of Sociology and Human Relations, Lucknow University, Lucknow, P. 13,1954.

Parsons, T. Essays in Sociological Theory, The Free Press, Glencoe. Illinois, 1958, p. 372.

Toren; Nina, Social Work: The Case of a Semi Profession, Sage Publications. Beverly Hills, London, 1972.

Tripody, Tony; Philip Fellen, Irwin Epskin, and Roger Lynd. An Introduction to Social Work Practice, Social Workers at Work, F.E. Peacock Publishers, Inc., ITASCA, Illinois, 1976, p.4.

U.G.C. A Review of Social Work Education in India: Retrospect and Prospect. Report of the Second Review Committee. U.G.C. Feb. 1978 (mimeographed).

Walla A. R., (1961). Ethical and Spiritual Values in the practice of Social Work" in A, R. Wadia, et al. (ed.), HiAtory and Philosophy of Social Work in India, Allied Publishers Private Ltd., Bombay, p. 3.

Wilensky, Harold L.: and Charles N. Lebeaux, (1958). Industrial Society and Social Welfare, Russell Sage Foundation, New York.

Wilensky, H. L. (1964). The professionalization of everyone? *American journal of sociology*, *70*(2), 137-158.

Witmer, I lelen L. (1942). Social Work: an analysis of an institution, Farrar and Rinehart Inc., New York.

4. NEED AND METHODOLOGIES FOR DEVELOPMENT OF KNOWLEDGE FOR PROFESSIONAL SOCIAL WORK PRACTICE IN INDIA

Prof. Surendra Singh[1]

Social Work as a professional service directed towards solution of psycho-social problems and introduction of desired changes in the social system to promote social development and reduce man - made inequalities, must have sound base of validated knowledge for its effective functioning. In other words must engage in the systematic pursuit of knowledge relevant for its practice. All Research in social work or Social Work Research (Dasgupta 1968; Khan in Jacob (ed.) 1994; Khan and Kakkar 2000; Bose in Khinduka (ed), 1962) must be geared towards generation of such knowledge as may be instrumental in promoting social work practice- remedial or developmental (in a developing country like India characterised by mass problems of) poverty, unemployment, illiteracy insanitation

[1] *Late; Head Department of Social Work, and former Pro Vice-Chancellor, Lucknow University*

inclusive of environmental degradation of varied kinds ill health, population explosion etc., the latter to be given a place of priority).

Social work research has no option but to evolve such methods and techniques as may be suited to the typical requirements of social work field. Ramchandran (1990) has rightly observed: "given the fact that the substantive area of interest of social work research in the whole canvas of social work practice, it is presumed, and rightly so, that this may require research strategies-generic and specific-which may have to be worked out to meet the specific peculiar conditions of social work field". Thus it is not out of greed for making social work 'look a respectable practice profession' (Ramchandran, 1987) but solely out of the dire necessity for promoting development of substantive and methodological knowledge without which effective social work practice is not possible that social work research has been accepted as one of the three auxiliary methods of social work.

Social work practice and social work research are inextricably linked with each other: the former helping in the identification of social work research problem (s) and the latter resulting in generation of knowledge for improved and better social work practice. The Report of the Workshop on Research in Social Work 1948 (cited in Hasan, 1971) clearly says: "in social work research the problem to be investigated is always found in the course of doing social work or planning to do it". Polansky (1960) has also clearly stated: "social work research begins with practical problems, and its objective is to produce knowledge that can be put to use in planning or carrying on social work programmes".

Hasan (1971) adds: "Social work is a profession, and therefore, research into the variables involved in practice, that is, in doing things with and for people-individually and in groups-should receive a great deal of attention".

Mohan (1986) goes still further and says: "the fact, however, is that social work research as an organised scientific endeavour is an established professional activity toward building up a general theory of human behaviour and social functioning involving a coherent system of interventions".

Social work research thus is an essential part of social work. It is a systematic pursuit of knowledge which leads to better understanding and improved practice. Like any scientific research, social work research also has two components: (1) Substantive and (2) Methodological. The first dealing with areas in which social work research is done, and the second concerning itself with methodological issues. As for the substantive component, Reid (1987) has pointed out: "The great bulk of Social Work research can be classified into the following categories: (1) studies concerned with the behaviour, personality problems and so on, of individuals, families and small groups, both client and non-clients; (2) investigation of the characteristics, utilisation and outcome of services; (3) research on the attitudes, orientations and training of social workers, on the social work profession or on interdisciplinary concerns; and (4) studies of organisations, communities and social policy". It is noteworthy here that research in methodology of social work research is also one of the most important areas (Hasan, 1971).

To achieve any goal effectively requires some methodological action which means an action characterized by method or order (Brown 1993). And this requires methodology which in the New Shorter Oxford Dictionary edited by Brown (1993) has been defined as "1: the branch of knowledge that deals with method and its application in a particular field. Also, the study of empirical research or the techniques employed in it...2: a body of methods used in a particular branch of study or activity".

In the context of social work research also, "development of methodology and tools for research is essential" (Goyal & Dasgupta (ed) 1967). Unfortunately lack of adequate research methodology has, from the very beginning, been a serious problem in Social Work research.

Long back Klein (1949) had unequivocally and clearly stated: "Social work by definition is meant to be practical, direct and comprehensible by beneficiary and practitioner alike and studies in research methodology often seem far removed from the day-to-day problems of providing service". And so did Greenwood (1951); "Lack of an adequate research methodology has been one of the factors hindering researches of other types, especially researches in practice and its results. In general research methodology, as a field of social work researches has received little attention with the result that most of social work research, is methodologically speaking of poor quality and even "questionable". Reid (1987) has also observed: "the philosophical and methodological foundations of social work research have been questioned by a number of critics...common themes in their arguments relate to the inadequacy of paradigms commonly taught, used and accepted by social work researchers". Realising this (Stuart 1971) has suggested that "a more refined methodology must be introduced into social work research".

Research in social work in India has been undertaken by social workers mostly social work educators or research scholars pursuing researches for M. Phil or Doctoral or Post-Doctoral degrees. The former, in addition to their own researches securing them one and/ or the other kind of degree(s) have also conducted researches sponsored by ICSSR, UGC, different Ministries/Departments of Government of India/State Government, particularly those dealing with matters related to social welfare, social security, social development etc. which have generally been descriptive and evaluative. It is noteworthy here that the studies conducted with a view to obtain degrees have not been very careful in respect of methodological issues. Not only the objectives and research questions have not been precisely specified but even the sampling plans have not been scientific, clarifications and tabulations have been improper, and analyses and interpretations have been logically as well as statistically unsound. In the quest for being scientific, various statistical methods and techniques have been used without properly understanding what they are or what they mean, what is the rationale behind their use, what kinds of conditions ought to be satisfied for their use, what are the basic premises on which they are based, what are the situations in which they should be used, and how the results obtained should be interpreted in order to arrive at correct conclusions. Quite a sizeable number of studies directed towards establishing some kind of association or correlation have been making use of concerned statistical devices such as Yule's Coefficient of Association (Q) Phi Coefficient (ϕ), Coefficient of Contingency (C), chi square Test of Significance (X2), Rank-Difference Method of Correlation (P), Karl Pearson's Coefficient of Correlations (r), Multiple correlation, regression, etc., without fully understanding their implications.

Social work in India being basically concerned with solving psychological and social problems and bringing about desired changes in the social structure and system, particularly by reducing socioeconomic inequalities and tackling mass social problems which confront people and lower down their quality of life, social work research at the substantive level has to concern itself with (i) identification of felt-needs and problems, and resources that are available or that can be possibly mobilised; (ii) diagnosis of main causes responsible for creation of these problems, (iii) understanding of politico economic and social-cultural context within which these problems emanate, (iv) knowledge of the personality profile especially the behavioural and adjustmental patterns of people who face such problems; and (v) incessant search for methods, techniques, strategies and approaches suitable for tackling them. At the methodological plane, social work research will have to address to the following major issues:

1. Clear-cut specification of objectives.

2. Framing of research questions that are to be answered in course of enquiry.

3. Enunciation of hypothesis (es), if any, clearly laying down the null and alternative hypotheses, the tenability of which is to be ascertained in the course of investigation.

4. Formulation of operational definitions of various terms used, particularly in terms of operations that are required for measurement, even if it is of the nominal level.

5. Decision regarding design- exploratory descriptive, diagnostic, ex-post facto, experimental that is to be followed.

6. Specification of sources - field or documentary or secondary sources that are to be tapped for collecting the required information.

7. Clarification of universe - the sampled as well as target universe, the former being one that is actually sampled, and the latter representing ideally the territory which the researcher intends his generalisations to cover i.e., "the domain to which

we eventually apply our knowledge or a universe in which the fraction of units are for one reason or another inaccessible to measurement, such as refusals or not-at-homes" (Mueller and Schuessler 1969).

8. Determination of sample size - Type of sampling to be used, stages of sampling involved and method of drawing representative sample, in case census study is not be undertaken.

9. Decision regarding approach to be adopted - survey approach, historical approach, comparative approach, case study approach, evaluative approach, participatory approach, development approach etc. that are aimed at creation of empirically based service approaches or intervention technology, etc.

In social work research the conventional quantitative approach has been criticised by many and qualitative approach that has long been part of such disciplines as Sociology and Anthropology (Filstead, 1970, Glaser and Strauss, 1967) have been advocated, perhaps because complex social phenomena can better be understood through words than through numbers (Reason & Rowen, 1981). However, the methodology for translating these ideas relating to qualitative research into practice could not be developed in detail. (Karger, 1983).

10. Development of appropriate tools - observation guide/schedule, questionnaire/test, interview schedule/guide etc. that may yield reliable and valid data.

11. Selection regarding method(s) to be used for gathering the required data in an objective manner, keeping in view the objectives, profile of respondents, type of design, nature of tools, and resources of command.

12. Development of suitable plan for classification and tabulation of data by following the well-established standard rules. In a number of researches, the social Work researchers and even senior social work educators have been found to be committing a blunder of showing the assumed independent variable through rows and dependent variable through columns.

13. Decision regarding the kind of an analysis - logical or statistical, and within the category of statistical analysis - descriptive or inferential and again, within the sub-category of inferential - parametric or non-parametric, that is to be done; and the methods and techniques of interpreting the results that have been yielded by the analysis.

14. Decision regarding the consumers of research results - professional Social workers and educators, students or practitioners, clients, non-professional providers of social and welfare services, social policy makers, welfare administrators or people in general because that becomes a major determinant of the kind of language and style of presentation of the entire research work.

15. Specification of implications for professional social work educators, field

practitioners and prospective social work researchers in particular and social policy formulators in general.

Social work, even after more than six decades of existence in India, could not achieve a professional status. Most shockingly, even many of those who are at the helm of affairs - politicians and bureaucrats, do not even know what social work is, perhaps because professionally trained social workers could not create a distinct identity of their own by demonstrating the tangible effects of their practice. There is no private practice, and whatever practice is being done, it is through the auspices of governmental or non-governmental organisations aiming at promoting the development or empowerment of weaker and vulnerable sections of society or at solving the psychological and social problems of people in general, irrespective of their religion, caste or class or gender background or through social movements directed towards safeguarding the interests of people who have become the victims of such crisis situations as have brought them to the level of destitution or who have been discriminated against and subjected to varied kinds of abuse and exploitation, and therefore, suffered from various types of socio-economic inequalities.

If social work has to flourish in India, it will have to demonstrate its effectiveness by evolving Such models, strategies and approaches through continuous research as may provide practical solutions to mass problems particularly by bringing about structural and systemic changes, and as may demonstrate the tangible effects by successfully tackling psychological (such as anxiety neurosis, depression, etc.,) and social (for example role conflict, family conflict, marital discord, inter-caste and inter-community tensions, etc.) problems. This will inevitably require that all social work research should have its roots in one or the other kind of psychological or social problem or social development issues and direct itself towards ascertaining the effectiveness of the already available solutions in dealing with them or towards evolving new solutions of these problems, always bearing in mind that the clients - individuals, groups or communities - want such solution of their varied kinds of problem as may bring about betterment and improvement in their quality of life and ensure prosperity and peace. Effective solutions are possible only when problems are correctly identified; their causes are properly discerned; social milieu (where especially the resources and social evils exist is properly understood); personality profile of the beneficiaries, particularly their strengths and weaknesses and hopes and aspirations is rightly assessed; and most appropriate intervention strategy is selected and put into practice. Sine qua non of all this is development of appropriate but simple and easy-to-handle measurement tools such as paper pencil, self-report measures, self-anchored seals, self-anchored seals, behavioural measures like client-self monitoring, collateral monitoring, and situational tests, in vivo assessment, and physiological assessment (Hudson and Thyer, 1987) and correct methods of analysis and interpretations.

In a nutshell, methodological issues must be given a very serious attention in social work research if the overall effectiveness of social work is to be improved to advance it towards the attainment of professional status in India. (Polansky, 1971) had rightly visualized and forecast "It seems likely that if there is to be an explosion of knowledge in the area of social work in next decades, it will have to come through organized research as it has in other fields".

References

Bose, A. B. (1962). Social work research. In S.K. Khinduka (Eds.). *Social work in India*. Sarvodaya Sahitya Samaj: Jaipur.

Brown, L. (1993). *The new shorter oxford dictionary* (Vol. 2). Oxford Clarendon Press.

Dasgupta, S. (1968a). *Methodology of social science research*. New Delhi: lmpesx India.

Dasgupta, S. (1968b). *Social work research encyclopaedia of social work in India* (Vol. 2). New Delhi: Publications Division, Govt. of India.

Filstead, W. J. (Ed.). (1970). *Qualitative methodology: first hand involvement with the social world*. Chicago, Ill: Markham Publishing.

Glaser, B.G. & Strauss, A.L. (1967). *The discovery of grounded theory: strategies for qualitative research.* Chicago: Aldine Publishing Co.

Goyal, C.P. (1967). Social work research in India. In Sugata Dasgupta (ed.). *Methodology of social science research.* New Delhi: India.

Greenwood, E. (1951). Recent Trends in Social Work Research. *Sociology and Social Research*, *35*(4), 250-259.

Hasan, S. Z. (1971). *Social work education and research in India.* Lucknow, Department of Sociology and Social work, Lucknow University.

Hudson, W. W., & Thyer, B. A. (1987). Research measures and indices in direct practice. In Anne Minhan et al. (eds). *Encyclopaedia of social work* (Vol. 2). Maryland: National Association of Social Workers.

Khan, M. Z. (1994). *Social work education in India: Retrospect and prospect*. Delhi: Himanshu Publications

Khan, M.Z. (1994). Inputs in Research. In K. K. Jacob (ed.). *Social work education in India: retrospect & prospect.* Himanshu Publications: Delhi

Khan, M. Z. & Kakkar, J. (2000). *Social work research in India: retrospect and prospects.* Paper presented at the National Seminar on

Social Work in the Twenty First Century: Challenges and Opportunities organized by the Department of Social Work Lucknow University, Lucknow.

Karger, H. J. (1983). Science, research, and social work: Who controls the profession? *Social Work*, *28*(3), 200-205.

Klein, P. (1949). *The contribution of research to the progress of social work.* AASW Pamphlet. The Contribution of Research to Social Work.

Mohan, B. (1986). Social work research-An innovative process. In Surendra Singh & K.S. Soodan (eds,). Honzons of Social Work, Lucknow.

Mueller, J. H. & Schuessler, K. (1969). *Statistical reasoning in sociology.* Calcutta: Oxford and IBH Publishing Co.

Polansky, N. A. (1960). *Social work research.* Chicago: The University of Chicago Press.

Polansky, N. A. (1971). Research in social work. In Robert Morris et al. (eds.) Vol. II. *Encyclopaedia of social work.* New York: National Association of Social Workers.

Ramchandran, P. (1987). *Research in social work. Encyclopaedia of Social Work in India*. New Delhi: Publications Division. Govt. of India.

Ramchandran, P. (1990). *Issues in social work research in India*. Bombay: Tata Institute of Social Sciences.

Reason, P., & Rowen J. (1981). *Human enquiry: A source book of new paradigm research* (Eds). Chichester England: John Wiley & Sons.

Reid, W. J. (1987). *Research in social work.* In Anne Minhanet. al. (Eds.), Encyclopaedia of Social Work Vol. 2.

Stuart, R. B. (1971). *Research in Social Casework and Social Group work.* In Robert Morris et al (eds), Encyclopaedia of Social work, Vol. II. op. cit.

5. THEORIES IN SOCIAL WORK VS. SOCIAL WORK THEORY: PREDICAMENT FOR PROFESSION AND INDIATIONS FOR POSSIBLE CURRICULUM CHANGE AND PRACTICE REORIENTATION

Prof. Rajeshwar Prasad[1]

Introductory

There is a plethora of theories in social work education, training, research and 'practice', and one may account for approximately thirty 'theories' taught during the period of instruction to social work graduates. These theories have been borrowed from other disciplines viz., psychiatry, psychology, sociology, anthropology, economics, criminology, political science, policy science, philosophy, administration etc. There is an exercise made by social work educators and practitioners in attempting to do a good-fit of these theories with 'professional practice.'

[1]*Late; Professor Rajeshwar Prasad was former Director, Institute of Social Services, Agra (India); has also been the President, ISPSW and Ex-Chairman. Indian Association of Social Science Institutions, New Delhi. He was the President, Indian Social Science Association.*

The 'theories' are taught in different courses/papers in a two-year Masters and/or the Master of Philosophy (M.Phil.) courses. From a perusal of social work courses in India it may be surmised that the theories are intangibly taught, which may be inferred from the fact that the 'objectives' of imparting theories to the students are not clearly stated by the schools/ departments, and that the teaching of theories is discrete and dispersed; it is evident from the fact that these are contained in different courses viz., social science for social workers; psychology for social workers; case work; group work; community work; social action; social research/social work research; social policy and administration; rural community organisation and welfare; medical and psychiatric social work/clinical social work; family and child welfare; correctional social work; etc. (the nomenclatures of courses of different schools do not conform to the ones enumerated here and mentioned in the syllabi thereof, but relate to the subject matter as such).

Theories taught and their sources

It may be fruitful to understand the different types of theories taught and the logic as to why are these imparted to the students. Instead of enlisting the different theories here, it may be logical to group these theories in broader categories e.g., theories of evolution; theories of personality (development) and learning theories; theories of social organisation and social change; theories of social stratification; theories of individual and group behaviour; theories of deviance, crime and correction; theories of economic growth and development; theories of group dynamics and leadership; theories of social work (clinical practice), etc.

For a comprehension of these theories there are innumerable books prescribed by the social work schools which pertain to different disciplines viz., psychology, sociology, political science, economics, criminology, etc. But, the theories imparted under the nomenclature of 'social work theories' which have a coveted place in the curriculum are contained in books with either same or similar title. We identified approximately eight books with either a prefix or suffix of ‘social work theories’ or theories related to its methods prescribed in the syllabi of different schools/ departments of social work in the country. These being: (i) Theory and Practice of Social Case Work by Gordon Hamilton (1951, Columbia University Press, New York), (ii) The of Social Work Practice by Ruth E. Smalley (1967, Columbia University Press, New York); (iii) Theory Building in Social Work by Gordon Hearn (1958, University of Toronto Press, Toronto); (iv) Learning Theory and Social Work by Derek Jehu (1967, Routledge, London); (v) Social Case Work Theories in Action by Herbert F. Strean (1971, Scarecrow Press, Metuchem, N.J.); (vi) Theories of Social Case Work by Robert W. Roberts and Robert H. Nee (1970, University of Chicago Press, Chicago); (vii) Social Work Treatment: Interlocking Theoretical Approaches by Francis J. Turner (1979, Free Press, New York); (viii) community Organisation: Theory, Principles and Practice by

Murray G. Ross (1995, Harper and Row, New York). Other books related with theories, not directly associated with social work but included in social work syllabi were : Towards a Theory of Rural Development by Hague N. Mehtra, A. Rehman and P. Wingnaraja (1975, National Institute of Data Management, Bombay); Theory and Methods of Social Research by J. Galtung (1967, George Allen and Unwin, London); Social Theory by J. Wilson (1983, Prentice Hall, New York); Social Theory by J. Wilson (1983, Prentice Hall, New York); Social Theory and Social Policy by R. A. Pinkar (1971, Heineman, London); An Introduction to Political Theory by C. J. Friedrich (1967, Jaico Publishing House, Bombay); Community Power and Democratic Theory by D. Ricci (1971, Randon House, New York), Counselling : Theory and Practice by H. B. Pepinsky and P. N. Pepinsky (1954, Ronald Press Co., New York).

Other books from the disciplines of psychology, sociology, anthropology, philosophy, economics, criminology etc., prescribed in different courses also discussed concepts, theories and models related with social work education. For examples, personality theories, learning theories, role theories, system theories, existential philosophy, deviance theories, growth/development theories etc., are contained therein. Also, host of other books on social work, social work philosophy, social work methods, and social work practice etc., dealt with the 'theories' associated with the professional practice/method.

The Report of the Curriculum Development Centre in Social Work Education of the University Grants Commission, recognised three organising elements of social work curriculum: (a) values of the profession; (b) the skills and the methods that are developed for the professional task, and (c) the major and concepts (U.G.C., 1990). The Report, acknowledging the importance of theories in social work curriculum avers that these are essential elements "to provide room to include newly developed knowledge to refine practice, and provide a continuing and also a changing theoretical base. In growing professions, it is also a well-known fact that some theory is available. While some is built up from the practice in the cause of meeting people's needs" (Ibid. p.30). As stated above, the syllabi of the schools/ departments not only contained various theories in discrete and dispersed manner but also did not state the objectives of teaching theories thus escaping from the question as to 'why do you teach theories to social work graduates.' However, the Report as above, does reiterate the functions of theory teaching as refinement of practice, the provision of changing theoretical inputs to the social work knowledge base, and building up of new theories from the 'practice-data'. The Repot has not discussed the nature of social/ social work theory. Nonetheless, it is imperative to note that the Report has also included many different theories discretely and dispersedly in different courses recommended by it to be pursued at the Bachelor's and Master's levels, rather than doing selectivity of appropriate theories to be taught rationally and as an independent course. Such compact courses are found in sociology, economics, political sciences, psychology etc. One many find courses and relevant books with captions viz., sociological theories; Modern economic Theories; Contemporary political Theories; Psychological Theories, etc.

Role of Theory in Social Professions

The term 'theory' is used loosely in social and behavioural sciences and also in the 'practice of social professions' as compared to its meaning and use in natural and physical sciences. The use of 'social work theories' in professional literature is rather ambiguous and sometimes the concepts, frames of reference, practice models and philosophical propositions have been termed 'theory (ies)'. Some social work practitioners maintain that due to the very nature of fast changing society - social relations, social institutions, culture, economy and polity, attitudes and behaviour patterns, dynamics of client-practitioner relationship and the very eclectic nature of the profession, theory has no value in professional practice. Whereas, others advocate the primacy of 'theory' in social work knowledge and practice. It must be theory, it is forcefully argued by many practitioners and educators, which should inform and guide practice and the 'practice' must function as feedback for theory reformulation. However, there is little appreciation of relationship between theory and practice of social work all over. It may be understood from the following exposition of theory and its place is social work.

What is Theory?

Geoff Payne et al. (1981) observed that from the positivistic angle "scientific theory should be something that goes beyond opinion or faith"; commenting further on the new theoretical developments they said that '... new theoretical developments are still born, and a premium is placed on theoretical disputation which operates without resource to the features of the external world'. Francis J Turner (1979) said that "the word theory is used to describe a logical explanation of the interrelatedness of a set of facts that have been empirically verified or are capable of being verified". Ken Menzies (1982) commenting on theoretician's theory and research theory in sociology averred that "... theories should arise from, feed into, be refined by and changed on the basis of research. The theory-research link legitimises sociologists' academic respectability". It is true of social work too. Without going into controversies I would only like to mention that theory building in natural sciences follows a set method and rigour; again, natural facts can be easily verified empirically while the social facts are dubiously identified and empirically verified with doubt and difficulty. In science it was not difficult to overturn Newtonian formulations by Einsteinian theory of relativity based on verifiable hypotheses, variables and propositions. Such theories are not either available or possible in social science. Since most social work theories are drawn from social and behavioural sciences it may be imperative to examine the nature of such theories in the light of above observations.

The Theory in Social and Behavioural Sciences

Jonathan H. Turner (1995) in The Structure of Sociological Theory says that "Theory is a mental activity... it is a process of developing ideas that can allow us to explain how and why events occur. Theory is constructed with several basic elements or building blocks: (1) concepts, (2) variables, (3) statements, and (4) formats". "...much of what is labelled sociological theory is, in reality, only a loose clustering of implicit assumptions, some basic concepts, and various kinds of theoretical statements and formats. But none of these is dominant or sufficiently precise to constitute a paradigm.... Thus, a great deal of 'theory' (in sociology) is really a general perspective or orientation for looking at various features of the social world" (Ibid, p. 32).

As already stated the very nature of social phenomenon prevents formalized theory formulation expressed either in a mathematical formula or a physical science analogue. M. Francis Abraham (1992) has aptly remarked that, "the social world and human behaviour within it are so complex that any simplistic model can only distort reality. This is not to argue that model building or measurement has no place in sociology. The point is that the contention that every social phenomenon must be quantified is neither acceptable nor desirable". It hold true of the status of theory in social professions including social work also.

The behavioural sciences on the other hand claim to be more 'scientific' precise and building 'true theory'. Francis Abraham while dealing with the Myth of True Theory averred that "In behavioural sciences, the quest for a true theory could be a futile intellectual exercise; every theory holds some pieces to the picture puzzle of the social world. A complete picture of social phenomena emerges only through the integration of a variety of social theories" (Ibid, p.17).

Social and behavioural scientists, obsessed as they are with the natural science model, have a 'theoretical bias' for explaining social events and behavioural expressions. This bias has led to the growth of variety of theories viz., (i) Speculative theories (an abstract impressionistic approach rooted in the philosophical system); (ii) Grounded theories (based on the findings of empirical research), (iii) Grand theory (broad conceptual scheme with systems of interrelated propositions that provide a general frame of reference for the study of social processes and institution(s); (iv) Miniature theories (partial or inclusive theories which Merton calls the theories of middle range); (v) Macro or Molar theories (broader in scope that encompass an extended range of laws); (vi) Micro or Molecular theories (narrow frame of reference and focus on a limited range of phenomena). It is in this context of the debate on the typology of theories in social and behavioural sciences that the issue of their utility in not only explaining the phenomenon but also the exact prediction of its change, has been raised time and again. Since these are not exhaustive theoretical formulations and deal with limited aspects of social phenomena they may be 'miniature' theories, and at time may be 'molecular' in nature. Social work 'theories' at best be categorised miniature and/or molecular.

Robert K. Merton (1968) has termed most theories of social science as Middle Range theories. Menzies rightly observes that "Middle range theory seeks to establish scientific laws about the impact of particular social factor on particular activities and avoids making comprehensive statements about society. It puts forward limited casual claims about specific social processes" (op. cit., p, 123). In social professions, a large part of practice is influenced by either miniature or middle range theories borrowed from social sciences or by molecular/micro theories developed in the profession itself. Many theories particularly in clinical settings have originated from an interface of particular factors with specific activities and thus are very restrictive in nature. The profession of social work is no exception.

Theories in Social Work vs. Social Work Theory

Noel and Rita Timms (1977) have aptly remarked that Theory is quite often used in social work in an ambiguous way, referring as it does to at least three possibilities: theory about what constitutes or justifies social work, theory about how to do social work and theory in the sense of propositions from, say, the social sciences. Turner (1979) in the Preface to the First Edition of the edited book Social. Work Treatment says that "In recent years the cry has been frequently raised that social work practice does not have an adequate theoretical base. Clearly, like all other professions practicing in the area of human adjustment, we do lack a sufficiently comprehensive and integrated body of theory necessary to understand and explain the myriad of situations we are called upon to assess" (Op. cit., p. xvii). Turner had planned this book with the caption, 'The Theoretical Bases of Social Work Practice', but soon it became clear that social work profession has been quite imprecise in the use of the word 'theory', the book was then titled "Social Work Treatment - Interlocking Theoretical Approaches and the topics included, although frequently designated, as theories, do not fulfil the requirements of the concept 'theory' (op. cit. p. xix-xx)."

Social Work has been widely viewed as a 'helping profession'. This helping thrust has been broadly classified into (i) clinical, and (ii) wider system-change orientation. The theories used in social work practice in the Western world viz., USA, Canada are predominantly individual pathology oriented, largely influenced by psychoanalytic theory, with far-fetched implications/ usage for group dysfunctional, community conflicts, family disintegration due to economic forces, and wider societal contradictions that are greatly responsible for individual maladjustments, group disorganisation, other social problems in any society.

The realization that problems of individual and/or group and community malfunctioning/ maladjustments, are rooted in the economic and social malaise created due to the inherent contradictions of the capitalist eco-political system, ultimately lead to the recognition of macro-analyses and the realization of the necessity of mega-actions. Hence, the importance of concomitant Marxist theories, still valid for understanding the social realities in the Developed and Third World Societies. It was given due consideration by some social workers also. These theories have guided practice of considerably good number of professional social workers in U.K., other European countries and Latin American societies. We will discuss both these types of theories and adjunct practice.

Chart depicting a comparative picture of various theories

Name of Theory And Theorist	Type and Discipline From where borrowed	Main Usage in Social Work	Any other Function
Psychoanalytic Theory --Sigmund Freud	- Interpretative and Therapeutic. Diagnosis and Therapy, *Psychiatry.	-- Widely used in Case Work. -- Individual Therapy.	-- No application for Group and Community problems.
Ego-Psychology --Post Freudians: Anna Freud; Heinz Hartman; Erik Erikson, etc.	-- Theory of Personality -- Recognises Ego's autonomous roots, development and function. -- Therapeutic. * Psychiatry.	-- Used in Case Work. -- Individual therapy orient	-- No application in Group malfunctio-ning and Community conflicts.
Psychosocial Therapy -- Began with Mary Richmond's	-- More an Approach and a thought system rather than a theory. -- Influenced by	-- Largely Individual oriented.	-- Limited application for family and other group problems.

recognition of `social' factors, and later given a thrust by Gordon Hamilton, Annette Garrett; Lusille Ausyin; Florence Hollis etc.	Psycho-analytic theory; ego-Psychology, sociological theories of Robert K. Merton and Talcott parsons and Anthropological theories especially of Clyde Kluckholn -- Therapeutic *Psychology		
Problem-Solving Theory -- Helen Harris Perlman; -- Barbara, J. Betz; -- D. Hallowitz; etc.	-- Not a 'theory', rather it is derived from many theoretical constructs. -- Concerned with individual's discrete problems. -- Such problems are consciously brought by the client and affirmed by the case worker. -- It is a conscious, focused, goal directed activity. * Leans on Social Psychological concepts	-- Used in Case Work. -- Individual oriented intervention. -- Focus on problem diagnosis, crisis intervention, correction of disparities, assertive counselling. -- Specific problem solving. -- Used in Case Work.	-- No use for community work. -- Focus on the Family. -- Not applied on other groups and community problems.
Functional Theory -- Jessie Taft; Virginia Robinson; Ruth Smalley; Kenneth Pray, etc. -- Widely influenced by the philosophy of Herbert Mead, John Dewey and Otto Rank -- University of Pennsylvania being the originating centre.	-- Therapeutic. -- Opposed to the diagnostic school, Psychoanalytic theory and Ego-Psychology. -- Treatment is replaced by the concept of 'Service.' -- Client/individual is perceived as an active agent rather, merely reactive in his own development. Use of AGENCY and agency-function in `service rendering' being very	-- Individual oriented intervention. -- Diagnosis is inextricably woven in the therapeutic process but the conceptualization of practice is seen in a broader perspective taking (i) psychological factors, (ii) social bases of the client, and (iii) functions of the Social Agency under whose ageism the	-- Not of any consequential application to the myriad problems of group mal-functioning and community disorders.

	important. -- Outcome of the concern of social workers to develop a 'legitimate theory' for social work practice. -- It is not a Theory in the strict scientific sense but a 'plan for action.' * Psychology and Sociology.	services are rendered. -- Used again in Case Work	
The Client-Centred Therapy [Also referred to as Relationship therapy; Group centred therapy; Person-centred therapy] -- Carl R. Rogers -- Virginia Axlines (Play Therapy)	-- Personal Counselling and Psychotherapy as basic components. -- Influence of Psychiatry. -- Non-directive, client centred -- Reference to present situation with no reference to past reactions. -- By its very nomenclature it is Therapy and the use of word Theory is in the sense of concepts used in therapy. * Clinical Psychology	-- Psychiatric social workers use it. -- It takes holistic and humanitarian view of man. -- Individual based, but 'helps individuals in groups.' -- Marital maladjustments also in eluded.	-- May be applied in Teaching, Training and Education in non-therapy situations. -- Also used to utilize, experiential learning in community formation, pro-cesses and meaning.
Cognitive Theory -- Alfred Adler -- Use in Social Work by -- Harold D. Werner. Also known as 'rational' psychotherapy' -- Robert Sunley (1968) was first to use the term 'Cognitive Case Work'	-- Approaches included are 'rational', 'reality' phenomenological -- It is socially oriented and believes that principal determinant of emotions, motives and behaviour is 'thinking' which in turn is influenced by society, immediate environment, human relationships and experience in general.	-- Individual therapy. -- Used in Case Work	-- It is argued that since cognitive theory is reality-oriented, it can serve as a guide to all forms of treatments: individuals, group and community. -- No evidence of its use in group/community maladjustments and conflicts.

	-- Discards element of unconscious --Existential, Functional theories have elements comparable with it. -- it is a 'clinical theory' -- Individual psychology of Alder; also associated with psychotherapy. * Psychology		
Gestalt Theory -- Fritz Pearls -- Laura Pearls -- Paul Goodman, etc.	-- Influenced by Psycho-analysis, Existential philosophy, Reichian Character analysis, Gestalt Psychology and traces of Eastern Religions. -- Central to Gestalt therapy is the use of the flow of conscious with the environment. -- Although contact with the client in the here and now situation forms the technique -- Gestalt therapy orients the worker toward encouraging the fullest expression of the client as a person. * Psychiatry & Social Psychology.	-- With philosophical roots in phenomenology and existentialism, Gestalt Therapy has offered a great deal to Social Work. -- Individual, therapeutic, stepped in Case Work	-- It is argued that due to the organismic nature of Gestalt theory, there is a close connections with systems theory and hence can be of use for macro microsystem. -- May be used in Group Work and Community Work. -- No evidence of such use.
Role Theory - Ruth Benedict - Kingsley Davis - William J. Goode - Ralph Linton - Florian Znaniecki **In Social Work** - Herbert S.	- Role signifies: Cultural Pattern; Social Norm, Basic factor in the process of socialisation; synonym as behaviour; participation in a specific group; carrying a status. -- Derived from	-- The notion of role prescription has been used in case work treatment. -- Again, it is individual oriented. -- It helps the worker also to delineate his role	-- Role theory emphasises on social interaction hence the client is not seen as a diseased entity; he is seen as a reflection of family system so its positive use in family therapy.

Strean - Helen Harris Perlman - Charles R. Atherton - Carol meyer	Sociology and Social Psychology -- It is largely used in conjunction with social system theory and also behaviour modification therapy. * Sociology/Social Psychology.	as catalyst, neutralizer, advocate, stimulator etc.	-- It is gainfully used in work with deprived groups and ethnic minorities -- Interpersonal problems in small groups and communities; role relationship are examined; and description, prescriptions and sanctions reviewed. -- Problem resolution is viewed as group and community task.
Behaviour Modification Technology -- Also termed as Action Therapy --Perry London -- B.F. Skinner etc.	-- An approach rather —than a Theory. -- Promote changes in client's behaviour di-erectly. -- Identify the target behaviour and control the antecedent conditions.... -- Consequences of behaviour may be assessed and interventions to avoid harm may be planned. * Psychology (Behaviourist School) and Psychiatry	-- Intervention with individuals. -- Dyadic i.e., Therapist-Client OR 'Triadic' - Therapist, Mediator and Client, work for modification	-- Environmental Engineering as secondary objective.
Family Therapy -- Structural Family Therapy -- Strategic Family therapy or -- Systems Therapy --Nathan W.	-- Not a theory -- Widely accepted in mental health and social service arena for practice. -- It is a shift from atomized level of individual to the level of family. -- Focus on family,	-- Family case work -- using subgroups such as the family dyads and triads. -- Ultimately it aims at improving social functioning, restores equilibrium,	but the individual person goes be-yond the family in the interdependent subsystems e.g. neighbour-hood, community, ethnic Subculture etc. — Other sub-systems are not

Ackerman --Virginia M. Satir --Salvador Minuchin, etc.	centres attention on the social psychological linkage between individual and larger social organization. -- Embedded in Sociological theories and Psychiatric Approaches. * Sociology, Social Psychiatry.	strengthen adaptation of individual persons.	taken care of.
Task-Centred Treatment -- William J. Reid -- Laura Epstein, etc.	-- Evolved from a model of brief, time limited Case Work. -- Psycho-social case work for helping individuals and families with problems in family relations. -- Clients define their psychosocial problems and have hope to solve these problems -- Reliance on tasks as a means of problem resolution. * Social Psychology	-- Help Individuals. -- Used in Case Work	-- The strategy may be applied to work with clients in families and `formed groups' assembled to help, individual members to solve their problems.
Crisis Theory Harvard School of Psychiatry and Public Health, and Benjamin Rush Centre of Los Angeles are its birth place. -- Howard J. Parad -- Lydia Rapport, etc	-- Derived from Case Work practice of Social Work. -- Crisis situations which disturb individual's homeostatic balance and put him in a vulnerable state thus heightening, anxiety, depression, deprivation, call for crisis intervention. -- Psychological models, sociological theories and social work practicc have influenced use of this 'approach.' -- Roots in	-- Medical situations generate crises and Medical Social Workers use it in their practice. -- Social/ Natural Disasters such as floods, hurricane and other such situations which uproot people and where social workers take work on the 'front line' may apply this approach. -- Immediate emotional first-aid and strengthening	-- Applied to correct family role net-works. -- Applied also to the friendship and common interest groups in crises

	psychodynamic personality theory, stress theory, learning theory, ego psychology, etc. * Psychology sociology and social work.	individuals coping capacity are its strategies.	
General Systems Theory -- L. von Bertalanffy -- W. Buckley -- G. Hearn -- H. Polsky -- I. Stein -- K. Rubin, etc.	-- There are living systems at the level of human individuals, groups, organizations and com-munities; they have certain characteristics in common. -- It is more a way of thinking, a way of viewing the world, than a theory. -- Instead of focussing on a system at one particular level, such as a group, it may take several levels, including the individual, the group, the organisation and the community. * Physical Sciences, Sociology	-- Used in practice/ methods. Human behaviour and the social environment; the 'core' systems and sub-systems (micro, mezzo, macro) are important in this theory.	-- Social welfare policy and services/ social work as a social institution; marital and family therapy; administration, organizational theory; field work.
Existential Social Work -- Soren Kierkegaard -- Dostoevsky -- Albert Camus -- Jean Paul Sartre (Compared with the Book of Ecclesiastes in Old Testament; Zen Buddhism in the East)	-- More philosophical perspective rather than specific technique or theory. --Impact on social work is unclear -- A Philosophy of despair and disillusionment. -- Impacted social work practice, yet less developed. * Borrowed from Philosophy, Religions/Theology.	-- Used for lessening categorization of people; cuts the paternalistic attitudes of therapists; more present-focused, experiential, task oriented, short term work with people	-- More effective treatment of the poor and minorities is expected with existential philosophical outlook.

Transactional Analysis (A social treatment model)--Eric Brene	-- People are born OK/I am Ok, You are Ok. -- People in social/emotional stress are capable of understanding their stress -- They want to be part of healing process and must be involved. -- All social/emotional difficulties are curable. -- Modelled in Social Psychiatry (may be termed alternative psychiatry). * Social Psychiatry	-- It fits with the ethics, goals, of social work for advocacy. Police are systems change towards social justice. In Social Work, TA offers an approach to client advocacy, policy planning and change. TA encourage self-management and responsibility for the quality of life.	-- TA can taught to administrators, legislators, and executives. So that they make the client/beneficiaries the participants in achieving healthy state of mind/action.
Meditation and Social Work Treatment [Arose from psycho philosophical systems of American Indians, Central Asian Sufi traditions; Chinese Taoism, Hindu Yoga, Buddhist and some Catholic Christian traditions, Jewish mysticism.]	-- Borrowed from theology, philosophy. -- It is by and large development of consciousness independent of visual and verbal symbols. -- Deliberate effort to cultivate mental state conducive to intuition. -- It may be used for stress release. -- It is also used as a therapeutic aid in psychiatry, (psycho-therapy) and social work. * Theology, Philosophy	-- In social work (also in psychotherapy) it is a method adjunctive to treatment. -- For those involved in social work treatment, the learnings transferred from meditation practice into the psychosocial functioning of the meditator may prove valuable.	-- Meditation may he used for 'release' and 'relaxation' of group of people.
The Life Model of Social Work Practice	-- Based on Ecological Theories	Since these are not found having a place in the syllabi on Indian Social work schools, these are not dealt here.	
Communication Concepts and Principles	-- Based on Communication Theories		

Note: The material abstracted in this comparative chart has been taken from the various articles contained in Social Work Treatment - Interlocking Theoretical Approaches, Francis J. Turner (editor) Second Edition 1979, Free Press, New York.

References

Abraham, M. F. (1982). *Modern sociological theory: An introduction*. Oxford University Press, USA.

Bernstein, H. (1976). *Underdevelopment and development: third-world today* (Eds). Penguin: Harmondsworth.

Bock, K. (1979). Theories of progress, development and evolution. In T.B. Bottomore & R. Nisbet (Eds). *A history of sociological analysis*. Heinemann: London.

Dantwala, M. L., Harsh S., & Pravind, V., (1988). *Social change though voluntary action*. Sage Publications: New Delhi.

Eisenstadt, S. N. (1970). *Readings in social evolution and development*. Pergamon Press Ltd: London.

Elsenhans, H. (1991). *Development and underdevelopment: the history, economics and politics of North-South relations*. SAGE Publications Pvt. Limited.

Frank, A. G. (1978). *Dependent accumulation and underdevelopment*. Macmillan: London.

Leonard, P. (1978). *Introduction to the series', in critical texts in social work and the welfare state- social work practice under capitalism: A marxist approach*. In Paul Corrigan and Peter Leonard (Eds.) The Macmillan Press Ltd., London.

Mayo, E. (1945). *Successful Vs. unsuccessful sciences in the social problems of an industrial civilization*. Harvar Business School: Boston.

Menzies, K. (1982). *Sociological theory in use*. Taylor & Francis.

Merton, R. K., & Merton, R. C. (1968). *Social theory and social structure*. Simon and Schuster.

Payne, G., Dingwall, R., Payne, J., & Carter, M. (1981). *Sociology and social rematch*, Routledge and Kegan Paul: London.

Prasad, R. (1980). Challenges of poverty and the social work curriculum. In R.R. Singh (ed.) *Social work perspective on poverty*. Concept Publishing Co.: New Delhi.

Roxborough, I. (1979). *Theories of underdevelopment*. The Macmillan Press Ltd.: London.

Statham, D. (1978). *Radicals in social work*. Routledge Kegan & Paul.

Takser, L. J.(1980). Practice and theory in community work. In Paul Henderson, David Jones and David N. Thomas (eds.). The *boundaries of change in community work.* George Allen and Unwin: London.

Timms, N., & Timms, R. (1977). *Perspectives in social work* (Vol. 1). Routledge.

Turner, F. J. (1979). *Theory and social work* treatment. *Social work treatment: Interlocking theoretical approaches*, *4*, 1-17.

Turner, J. H., & Turner, P. R. (1978). *The structure of sociological theory.* Homewood, IL: Dorsey Press.

University Grant Commission. (1990). *The Report of the Curriculum Development Centre in Social Work.* U.G.C.: New Delhi.

Walla, J. M. S. (1991). *Democratic Ethos and Developmental Process in India.* Uppal Publishing House.

About the Authors

Prof. Koteswara Raju (PhD) is currently working as the principal at National Institute of Social Work and Social Sciences (NISWASS) Odisha. He graduated from Andhra University, Visakhapatnam. Attained Doctoral Degree from Andhra University. Recipient of Meritorious teacher Award from Government of Andhra Pradesh. Recipient of outstanding abstract award for the Paper on Social Work Leadership in India at Hong Kong. Received fellowship from George Institute of International Health, University of Sydney, Australia. He is the former Principal of DNR Autonomous College, Bhimavaram, Andhra Pradesh. He is the founder, Academic Coordinator, of Department of Social Work at Central University, Kasaragod, Kerala. Founder of Vocational Guidance Bureau, College community network centre and Centre for extra-mural studies and lifelong learning. He has been a active life member of ISPSW and serve e the society in various capacity.

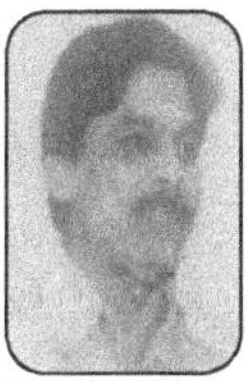

Late Prof. M. Chandrasekhara Rao (PhD) was the Additional Professor, at the Department of Psychiatric Social Work, National Institute of Mental Health and Neuro Sciences (NIMHANS), Bangalore. He has contributed his services in community mental health and subsequently worked intensively in the area of psychogenic depression and casework intervention for individuals suffering from depression in the clinical mental health setting. He was associated with more than 15 Universities is member of Academic Councils, Boards of Studies, Boards of Examiners, Selection Committees and PhD evaluations. He has prepared several TOT training manuals in the area of HIV for Hindustan Latex Family Planning Promotion Trust (HLFPPT). He has also guided several doctoral research studies in the area of child protection, life skills, psychosocial disability management with persons with schizophrenia and depression in the Institute. He has bagged several awards for his contribution to the field of community mental health. He was well known as a great teacher, trainer, educator, researcher, role model and mentor.

Late Prof. Rajeswar Prasad (PhD) was the Professor Emeritus and Former Director, Institute of Social Sciences, Agra, U. P. He has also been the President, ISPSW and Ex-Chairman. Indian Association of Social Science Institutions, New Delhi and President, Indian Social Science Association.

Dr. Prasad Studied in University of Lucknow, Department of Studies in Social Work, Obtained his Masters degree in the year 1959. Immediately after that he joined the Institute of Social Sciences Agra University as Assistant Professor under the guidance of stalwart Prof. Saxena, the famous sociologist. He became the Director of the Institute of Social Sciences, Agra and continued his services and retired as Professor in the same institution. After retirement he worked as professor in Rural Development Institute at Allhabad for quite some time.

He was an excellent teacher in Social Work, versatile Orator and travelled many countries in the World and he represented India in many conferences, seminars and workshops. He contributed his services for the development of profession and he was Editor for Indian Journal of Social Research. He brought out many scientific papers in both National and International Journals. He was Director/Investigator for locally and centrally sponsored projects. He was elected as third President of Indian Society of Professional Social Work and was associated with the Society throughout his life.

Late Prof. Surendra Singh (PhD) was former Vice-Chancellor of Mahatma Gandhi Kashi Vidyapith, Varanasi and former Pro Vice chancellor and Head of Department of Social Work, University of Lucknow.He was the Ex. Director, J.K. Institute of Sociology and Human Relations, Lucknow University. He is the Edior-in-Chief of Encyclopaedia of Social Work in India series. He was the President of ASSWI and founder President of NAPSWI. Prof Singh had passed B.A in 1962 and M.S.W.in 1964 with 1st division. He was appointed as Lecturer in 1964, Reader in 1978 and Professor in 1985.During his service, he continued his pursuit of education and acquired LL.B., Ph.D. and D.Litt. degrees from University of Lucknow itself. Diploma of N. D. Sc., M.D. in Alternative Medicine and D.Litt. were obtained from various other institutions.

Prof. K Satyanarayana is working a Prof. of Social Work & Principal, KGRL College, Bhumavaram, (A.P.). He awarded his PhD from Andhra University in 2001. He was awarded as best teacher award in the year 2003 by Government of Andhra Pradesh and best NSS programme officer in the year 1996 by west Godavari district collector. He is the member of professional bodies like ASSWI, ISPSW, and NAPSWI.

Late Prof. B R K Raju was the Professor of Social Work, in Andhra University, Visakhapatnam. He was a Former Adviser, Youth Affairs (Ministry of HRD Govt. of India) and National Services (Government of India). He was the President of Chaitanya Bharathi (a non-governmental organisation). Prof. B. R. K. Raju received M.A. (Ateneo De Manila), M.A.(S.W.), Ph.D (A.U).

About the Editors

Dr. Kamlesh Kumar Sahu has done Ph.D. from Calcutta University, Master of Philosophy in Psychiatric Social Work (M. Phil. PSW) at Central Institute of Psychiatry, Ranchi, Master and Bachelor from Ranchi University. He has more than 17 years of experience in the Mental Health field as a Psychiatric Social Worker. Currently, he is working as an Associate Professor in-charge of Psychiatric Social Work at the Department of Psychiatry, Government Medical College and Hospital, Chandigarh, India His experience includes teaching and supervision of postgraduate trainee, planning, execution, evaluation and coordination of counselling/mental health/ psychosocial rehabilitation services and research. More than 60 publications are in his credit in international and national journals of repute and he has presented papers in international and national seminars and conferences. Supervised 19 M. Phil. dissertations and completed two funded projects. His area of interest includes brief psychosocial interventions, psychosocial rehabilitation, and stigma alleviation.

Dr. Kamlesh Kumar Sahu is the Hon. General Secretary, Indian Society of Professional Social Work formerly non as Indian Society of Psychiatric Social Work (ISPSW). He is successfully transformed the National Journal of Professional Social Work from a conventional journal to an open access peer-reviewed, indexed journal as an editor. He is the Editor in Chief of Indian 'Journal of Psychiatric Social Work' which published first in 1972 at Central Institute of Psychiatry. He received Editorial Excellence Award 2018 by International Institute of Organized Research (I2OR) for his significant editorial contribution. Founder executive editor of Journal of

Disability Studies; section editor of a PubMed indexed Indian Journal of Psychological Medicine. He has also serving as an editorial board member and reviewer in more than 10 journals. He is very keen on scholarly publications, particularly open access publications. He has successfully upgraded and transformed many conventional journals into open access modern journal. He is a recipient of the Preeminent Researcher and Educator Award 2019 by Green ThinkerZ; 5th South Asian Education Awards 2020 for Research in Excellence. Instrumental in organizing various international and nation conferences; recently organized various webinars.

Dr. Chittaranjan Subudhi is working as an Assistant Professor, in Department of Social Work, Central University of Tamil Nadu Thiruvarur, India. He has done Master in Social Work from the Utkal University of Odisha, India and Ph.D. from the Department of Humanities and Social Sciences, National Institute of Technology (NIT) Rourkela, India. He has conducted research in various areas like Health and Mental Health, Medical Anthropology, Family and Child Welfare, Disability studies and Tribal Health issues. He has written many articles including conference papers and published in reputed national and international peer reviewed journals including Springer, Sage, Routhledge, Taylor & Francis and other SCOPUS indexed journals.

www.ingramcontent.com/pod-product-compliance
Lightning Source LLC
Chambersburg PA
CBHW062143160726
48282CB00027B/918
* 9 7 8 8 1 9 5 2 2 3 4 4 2 *